Management Accounting: retrospect and prospect

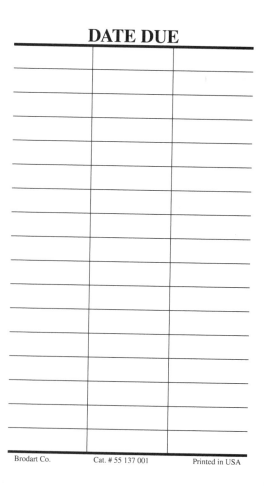

Management Accounting: retrospect and prospect

Alnoor Bhimani

and

Michael Bromwich

AMSTERDAM • BOSTON • HEIDELBERG • LONDON
NEW YORK • OXFORD • PARIS • SAN DIEGO
SAN FRANCISCO • SINGAPORE • SYDNEY • TOKYO

CIMA Publishing is an imprint of Elsevier

CIMA Publishing is an imprint of Elsevier
The Boulevard, Langford Lane, Kidlington, Oxford, OX5 1GB
30 Corporate Drive, Burlington, MA 01803, USA

First edition 2010

British Library Cataloguing in Publication Data
A catalogue record for this book is available from the British Library

Library of Congress Cataloging in Publication Data
A catalog record for this book is available from the Library of Congress

ISBN: 978-1-85617-905-8

For information on all CIMA Publishing publications visit our
website at books.elsevier.com

Transferred to Digital Printing in 2009

Working together to grow
libraries in developing countries

www.elsevier.com | www.bookaid.org | www.sabre.org

ELSEVIER   BOOK AID
International   Sabre Foundation

Contents

Preface

This is the third in a series of books which we have written that have been commissioned by the Chartered Institute of Management Accountants (CIMA). This book is part of the celebrations to mark CIMA's 90th anniversary in 2009. As is fitting, this book first looks at the development of cost and management accounting from the founding of the Institute to the current time. Secondly, it considers a number of immediate challenges to management accountants and surveys a number of issues and challenges that will likely affect management accounting thought and practice and the work of management accountants. This book builds upon two earlier publications by us sponsored by CIMA: *Management Accounting: Evolution not Revolution* (1989) which evaluated the then promise of a variety of emerging management accounting innovations including Activity Based Costing (ABC) and *Management Accounting: Pathways to Progress* (1994) which sought to consider 'approaches which may help expand the accountant's role in a dynamic and turbulent environment embodying increasing global competition...' This book reflects the current and future status of management accounting, and expands on the earlier books by focusing on what we believe are likely to be very significant changes in the business environment, including management accounting in a time of financial crisis, accelerating globalisation and fast-paced technological change and speculates on other factors that may burgeon and affect the accountant's role.

The history of cost and management accounting from the Institute's founding in 1919 spans cost bookkeeping geared to the valuation of inventory and for guiding pricing, the general establishment of the foundation techniques of management accounting, such as standard costing and budgetary control in the 1950s and 1960s and discounted cash flow capital budgeting in the 1970s, to accounting geared to decision support and management control using approaches such as strategic management accounting (SMA), value added methods, balanced scorecards (BSC), activity based costing (ABC) and its variants, and a variety of performance measurement systems. This history is important in understanding management accounting today as there is substantial evidence that accounting innovations often are not accepted or are very slow to achieve widespread acceptance and moreover that they are linked to a wide array of influencing conditions and forces. Thus for example, it took some 20–30 years for standard costing and budgetary control to gain extensive acceptance. The notion of standards of performance itself has a much more protracted history. The take-up of more recent innovations, such as ABC and BSCs has a lag of some 10 years approximately but adoption across industries and services has been quite variable. There is also strong evidence that extant management accounting systems remain traditional, often employing quite dated techniques in a substantially changed world subject to likely greater volatility.

It may seem inappropriate to presume the possibility of changes to come in the field in the midst of a possibly lengthy major recession where there is a clear call for accountants to use their well-practiced techniques to aid in downsizing and cost containment and financial discipline. We believe however that times of retrenchment and economic slowdown present possibilities and opportunities to effect change and engage in reflection of a degree which surpasses that likely to take place under more stable economic conditions of growth and expansion. The present is a time that allows creativity and alternatives to be posited and experimented with such as to redirect management accounting to paths otherwise unlikely to be explored.

This book looks at the possibilities for accountants to widen their focus to become much more familiar with enterprise technology which determines the firm's cost structure and with the effects of multi-product production in multi-locations such as economies or diseconomies of scale flowing from larger volumes and (dis) economies of scope generated by producing large product portfolios marketed and produced globally. This may require traditional cost models used by accountants to be altered and to become more nuanced. We suggest how this may be accomplished. One requirement that arises here if accountants are to understand enterprise technology and marketing strategy is that they need to work closely as business partners where accountants work as part of management teams throughout the organisation rather than remain grounded in specialist information provision roles.

With regard to the possible changes we see these as:

■ Both an acceleration of uncertainty as well as growing uncertainty about volatility across enterprise environments. This means that assumptions, projections, prognostications and information analysis now takes place with different expectations and objectives. It is the management accountant's obligation to assess the propriety of continuing with the status quo.

■ The rise of firms that are fluid in terms of technologies they use and in terms of mutable boundaries between them and suppliers and customers rejecting traditional management and governance structures, and strictly legal relationships with suppliers and, indeed, with customers.

■ Firms are likely to abandon the traditional logic that is part of the industrial era with its focus on the a priori conceptualisation, design and testing of products before production. Marketing and sales functions then account for and enable customers access to the product. The present day context for many firms entails instead, within many industrial, service-based and digital products, direct involvement by the customer in input and design. This occurs sometimes with products being separated from the associated source of revenue.

- Concerns which in a world of extreme volatility and novel contingencies will be questioned and potentially lead to the reshaping of management accounting. Collaborative alliances, virtual organisations and fluid structuring and other enterprise related forms provide a focus also for dealing with globalisation.

- Transparency and compliance stipulations with growing regulatory requirements are increasingly affecting enterprises. Management accounting will have to address issues of risk management and the design and implementation of appropriate governance mechanisms in the near term. Additionally, the growing concerns with sustainable business practices and environmental concerns will make demands for effective record capture and reporting approaches. Requirement for information of this novel type will be as much about communicating legitimacy of activities as about enabling bases for action.

We argue that these factors call for management accountants to develop an understanding of wider forces of change as well as of technical and organisation specific factors. Ultimately, the ability of management accountants to understand other areas of organisational functioning and other business models, and to integrate this emerging knowledge with the work, tasks and objectives of the changing management accounting function, will be a key factor in the profession's survival and continued growth. The field must continue to retain adeptness in recognising the significance and nature of emerging change as it evolves.

Acknowledgements

Our appreciation extends to the business executives, consultants and researchers who gave their time generously to assist in this project, and to the anonymous reviewers drawn from a variety of backgrounds. We also wish to express our gratitude to Kim Ansell, Head of Innovation at CIMA, and to her staff including Naomi Smith and to the copy editing skills of Clare Donnelly. We are very grateful to CIMA's General Charitable Trust for funding this project. The secretarial and typing skills of Ann Cratchley have been especially appreciated as always. We are also grateful for the assistance of Livia Radulescu in assisting with the bibliography.

About the Authors

Alnoor Bhimani is Professor of Management Accounting and Head of the Department of Accounting at the London School of Economics (LSE). He possesses an MBA from Cornell University where he was a Fulbright Scholar, and he holds a PhD from LSE. He is also a Certified Management Accountant (Canada). He is author of 15 books and over 100 articles. His books entitled *Management Accounting: Pathways to Progress* (CIMA, 1994), *Strategic Finance* (Strategy Press, 2008) and *Management and Cost Accounting* (FT/Prentice Hall, 2008) are best-sellers, with translations in several languages including French, Dutch, Italian, Portuguese, Japanese, Arabic and Mandarin. Al has also edited several books with Oxford University Press on management accounting, which continue significantly to influence research thinking in the area. He is an editorial board member of numerous established scholarly journals. He has undertaken strategy, financial management and control related research in a variety of global enterprises and has presented his findings to corporate executives and academic audiences in Europe, Asia and North America.

Michael Bromwich was CIMA's Professor of Accounting and Financial Management at the London School of Economics from October 1985 until 2006, now Emeritus. After qualifying as an accountant with the Ford Motor Company, he has taught in a number of UK universities. He has been for many years the Convener of a research group on management accounting research sponsored by CIMA and the ICAEW. He teaches both management accounting and financial corporate reporting. He was voted ACCA/AA Distinguished Academic of the year in 1999. He is a Past President of CIMA (1987/1988) and currently serves on CIMA's Technical Committee and was awarded the Institute's Gold Medal in 2009. He has written a number of books, including *The Economics of Capital Budgeting* (1976) and *The Economics of Accounting Standards Setting* (ICAEW, 1985). His most recent books are *Financial Reporting, Information and Capital Markets* (Pitman, 1992), *Management Accounting: Pathways to Progress* (CIMA, 1994) and, with others, *Following the Money: The Enron Failure and the State of Corporate Disclosure* (AEI-Brookings Joint Center for Regulatory Studies, 2003) and *Worldwide Global Reporting: the Development and Future of Accounting Standards* (OUP, 2006).

Executive Summary

1 Then, Now and the Future

This report provides a short review of the state of management accounting research and practice in terms of the brief by the Chartered Institute of Management Accountants (CIMA) that it:

> *will look at where the profession has been, what is its current state as CIMA reaches its 90th birthday and will prompt thought about where management accountancy is heading in the future with emphasis on the future of the profession in the light of globalisation, the increase in virtual organisations and the changing role of the management accountant.*

The book builds upon two earlier publications by us sponsored by CIMA: *Management Accounting: Evolution not Revolution* (1989, *ER* below) which evaluated the then promise of a variety of emerging management accounting innovations especially Activity Based Costing (ABC) and *Management Accounting: Pathways to Progress* (1994, *PP* below) which sought to consider 'approaches which may help expand the accountant's role in a dynamic and turbulent environment embodying increasing global competition...' All three reports provide major pointers to finance directors and chief financial officers as to ongoing trends, emerging challenges and possible opportunities for change acknowledging that historically any major dispersion of management accounting innovations is generally slow. Chapter 1 indicates that formal management accounting systems, to a large degree, continue to be structured along traditional routes in many enterprises. But firms desirous of change, now face options and possibilities for altering their management accounting systems given the implications of the increasingly global, digital and volatile environment faced by enterprises.

PP commenced by looking in some detail at a wide range of then current and emerging challenges facing organisations and management accountants and examined their implications and possible responses. It first considered the strong pressures to automate production activity with the introduction of numerical control devices, computer aided design and manufacturing and flexible manufacturing. Chapter 3 of this report, *Management Accounting: Retrospect and Prospect* (*R&P* below) indicates that this area of innovation has since exploded to such an extent that many firms today can technologically adopt a 'fluid and flexible' form in the face of the pressures of global integration, information exchanges and worldwide competition from production bases located across the globe and serviced by complex supply chains which themselves span locations around the world. 'Fluid organisations' were seen only on the horizon in *PP* in 1994 (see *R&P* Chapter 5). As they continue to rapidly evolve and develop, fluid and flexible firms will lead accountants to seek solid grounding in knowledge about the technology available to and deployed by the firm. Management accountants, it is anticipated, will aim to become skilled in appraising the benefits, costs and contextual issues of different customer supply networks and supply chains and report appropriately on the performance of such structures.

It is argued also that, the traditional and conventional view that comprehensive planning and decision making should precede operational action may falter as there is evidence from firms today that decision objectives often emerge during the process of operations and that decisions may be made whilst operational actions and production activities evolve in practice. It is thus the case that action is at times subsumed in assessments of information. Here management accountants will possibly seek to tie information from operations into reformulating decision models. Variances from plans may come to be seen as learning devices about the engagement of action and concurrent decisions rather than as instruments of formal responsibility accounting.

Aside from reassessing conventional thinking about management accounting systems design where it is assumed that managers think about and evaluate information prior to making decisions and taking action, in many enterprises non-formal information evaluation may be very significant in determining organisational endeavours. Additionally, appeal to information following the making of decisions often exists as a legitimacy endowing ritual. As enterprises increasingly operate in contexts of rapid change and extreme uncertainty, the assumed structured logic of information usage and decision making has to be questioned and reconsidered just as the use of non-formal information and the value of legitimacy endowing information deployment must be taken into account.

Around the time of publishing *PP*, the very strong pressure from consultants and some professional bodies to adopt ABC was probably at its height. At this time there were many passionate pleas to revolutionise management accounting by the wholesale adoption of ABC and its variants Activity Based Budgeting and Activity Based Management. This revolution has not come to pass (*R&P* Chapter 1). Various estimates of the take-up in economically developed countries have been made but 20% by large firms is a reasonable estimate of the upper range of take-up and is not surprising given the rigorous assumptions underlying ABC and the expense of implementing ABC. ABC can now be presumed as being potentially part of the accountant's tool bag having contributed to a degree, to our understanding of some overheads.

Chapter 1 of this book augments the consideration of many earlier developments in management accounting by considering a number of more recent innovations. For example, maximisation of shareholder value has been the publicly avowed objective of almost all firms though how this is enacted differs among firms. It is likely that these claims will become more muted in the current environment and that explicit corporate objectives may be expanded to encompass more stakeholders. Economic value management systems, such as economic value added (EVA$^{©}$), are now used quite substantially by the larger international firms (Chapter 1). These systems convert accounting results into economic ones by applying an interest charge on the book value of assets to accounting profit. This incentivises managers to select projects that earn 'super profits'. The evidence is that relatively few firms link managerial incentives explicitly to economic value management systems. Some firms have abandoned these approaches because of their perceived failure to capture the full richness of corporate performance. The other major problem associated with these methods is the difficulty of ensuring that the yearly performance measure correctly signals the lifetime performance of the project.

The creation of fluid and flexible organisations has been enabled by recent major changes in relationships with suppliers which have altered the traditional approach of seeking suppliers by formal legal and fully specified tenders and the substitution of supplier partnerships involving new substantial information exchanges between parties aided by digital technology including full knowledge of both the cost structures and production activities of all parties.

Trusted suppliers in such relationships may participate in the purchasing organisation's planning and may contribute to designing both the production technology and the products of the purchasing firm. In supply partnerships, management accountants may design information systems that allow more ready exchange of information between parties than has been the case in conventional contracting where extensive information is required of suppliers with purchaser information being kept private. They also have to become comfortable with operating in regimes having less formal management and governance structures than is traditional and rely more extensively on trust between partners whilst still providing appropriate performance reports.

Fluid and flexible firms founded on a strong digital platform experience new ways to deal with customers by enabling them to directly establish their preferences concerning product design, processing and capabilities and inserting these into the products to be consumed (*R&P* Chapter 4). For long, successful companies have been less inclined to invent entirely new products and services without interrogating consumers. But now, a large number of enterprises construct platforms allowing customers direct access to product creation and to collaboration infrastructures. Enterprises may co-create their products with the customer or they may go further and allow total product creation by the customer providing them a platform for doing so and thereby also enabling the generation of new consumer experiences in the process. Although enterprises may not pre-design the consumer experience with the product, they still invent the broad product concept and orchestrate the achievement of the product's potential via the consumer. A variety of industrial, service-based and digital products are created directly via customer input and design.

In electronic platform contexts, content of the website is generated by the consumers but it is the advertisements on the interactive platforms between users that form the revenue source. In these contexts, pricing and costing issues do not follow a traditional model which may be cost-plus based or market based. Rather, the pricing has to directly link into the strategy of the firm and its revenue generating model where the product that is costed does not directly align with where sales are generated. Co-creation of products is not a choice but a necessity for many business models because the product choices are infinite and cannot be conceptualised or delivered by one 'producer' and because the product created by the consumer is often not in fact the product that is ultimately generating the firm's revenues. Management accountants have a new role here in determining the costs and profitability of satisfying each of the specific preferences of consumers. That is, costing the product attributes developed with or by consumers and seeking to also analyse plausible revenue propositions that may be dissociated from the consumer created products.

Fluid organisations can assume different forms by definition. They can be informal grouping of firms or parts of firms seeking to achieve a specific shared objective(s). Such groups emerge when the legal, managerial and governance structures of the parent firms are altered to allow the group to act 'smart and quick' in a dynamic environment and to allow more immediate entrepreneurial or innovative activity. The founding of such groups may be to allow accessing of skills not possessed by some of the parent firms, developing new skills, forming a portfolio of skills so as to move into novel areas of activities, risk bearing, financing and planning projects too large for the individual founding entities of the group and to allow new products to be created that are otherwise unlikely to appear.

Fluid organisations are founded not on traditional conceptions of corporate structures but are bound together by shared endeavours and continuously orchestrated interfacing. This is one area where in order to contribute, management accountants will seek to be seen as part of management and operational teams and thus to become business partners. Management accountants will act possibly as the financial advisors or business partners to teams and will need to understand the technology underlying the organisation and learn to cope in such organisations without, at least, some of the conventional formal management control structures or systems. This role will naturally come to be combined with reporting to parent entities (*R&P* Chapter 5).

The emergence of accountants as business partners is a major possible innovation extending to many large firms (*R&P* Chapter 5). The early evidence is that this is welcomed by operations managers, who see business partners as being 'on their side' and by the accountant business partners themselves as they seek to engage in operational activities and to having a wider role than traditional management accountants of the same level.

One area which will likely pose challenges is in attaining balance in the responsibilities of the business partner to the team manager and to the accounting division. Perhaps, this problem will be tackled contextually and informally with some realignment of line responsibilities (*R&P* Chapter 5). Some enterprises are experimenting with business partners from other disciplines.

Virtual organisations represent a different form of fluidity extending far beyond the concept of outsourcing, strategic alliances or joint ventures because of their reliance on digitised platforms of operation and coordination. The virtual firm is an agglomeration of multiple 'buy' transactions weaved together by extensive technological structuring and managerial action coordination. Cost analyses are likely to entail many factors reflective of the complexities such an agglomeration brings together. A virtual enterprise is ultimately a goal-orientated arrangement between several firms or units of firms which temporarily assembles competencies and capabilities wherever they arise. There is linkage by information technology to share skills, costs and access to one anothers' markets. These are prime areas for the development of the management accounting function which are only now emerging for many firms.

A major thrust of *PP* (1994) was to examine and evaluate a number of then innovative cost management approaches. The further evolution of these approaches is charted in Chapter 1 of this report. Total quality approaches and Just-in-Time systems are now relatively extensive in many competitive contexts. Strategic Management Accounting and some of its approaches are reviewed in Chapter 2. Chapter 2 also considers modern methods of dealing with fixed overheads focusing on the treatment of joint costs. Chapter 4 of *PP* provides a more comprehensive treatment of this subject. It is notable today that the Balanced Scorecard and its variants are much used though the depth of application varies. In many companies, management accountants are responsible for consolidating the information for the balanced scorecard and publicising it within the organisation. This role requires accountants to cooperate with other functions in the firm who 'own' the non-financial information in the balanced scorecard. The use of the scorecard has moved over time from being a strategic performance system to a scorecard for some firms which seek to implement strategy through communication, developing action plans and as a basis for incentives. More developed applications are mostly still at early stages. There remains considerable evidence that firms tend not to take a fully balanced view of the information provided, often concentrating on financial information and often considering information not readily amenable to capture in simplistic balanced scorecard terms. As with many managerial innovations, it may be difficult or impossible to quantify the benefits of the balanced scorecard in financial terms. Many critics raise questions about any benefits accruing from its use.

CIMA introduced a 'strategic scorecard' to extend on the balanced scorecard concept whereby strategy is sought to be linked to governance issues (see Chapters 1 and 4). The CIMA Strategic Scorecard ^{TM} attempts to report on strategic position, strategic options, strategic implementation and strategic risks. It is too early to evaluate its likely take-up but it may fill an information gap for some enterprises.

One important alteration in management accounting in practice is the re-engineering, restructuring and downsizing of the finance function (*R&P* Chapter 1). This endeavour was born and developed by firms with some assistance from consultants. Much of this has become possible because of changes in computerised information systems and alterations in communication platforms. It is likely that such efforts will be redoubled in the current economic environment but there are core competences relating to finance which some enterprises will be reluctant to lose. Beyond this, transparency and compliance requirements with growing regulatory requirements will impinge on enterprises. This may put pressure on enterprises' information and control functions and perhaps extend the finance function's role in new directions. Management accounting will have to address issues of risk management and the design and implementation of appropriate governance mechanisms. Additionally, the growing concerns with business sustainability issues will make demands for record capture and reporting approaches being seen as legitimate.

Increasingly, regulatory environments adopt and operate in standardised forms. This is to a degree because transparency is regarded as enhanced due to the preference for commonality of approach to measurement, valuation and financial representation. Consequently, the management accountant needs to judge how economic flows can be represented in a manner reconcilable with external demands for global uniformity.

This book departs from *PP* in that there are no country case studies in this report considering management accounting developments in selected countries. This is in part because of the global nature of financial management and control issues. But also, because of a growing focus on knowledge interactions and development rather than geographical boundaries driving change.

As organisations become more knowledge management orientated, it is argued that the focus may turn to enhancing some notion of returns on people rather than maximising capital returns. This will sponsor the creation of organisations that seek to continuously adapt and evolve in line with knowledge input. If traditional structures give way to fluid enterprise designs and organisational forms which rest on expertise and knowledge creation potential, then the management accountant will have rethink organisational control approaches.

In sum, this book reflects on the current and future status of management accounting, focuses on emerging contemporary issues, including management accounting in an environment of accelerating globalisation, fast-paced technological change, financial crisis challenges and speculates on other factors that may burgeon and affect the accountant's future role.

2   Structure of the Book

A brief summary of the report is:

Chapter 1 Management Accounting: Past and Present
Provides a review of state of cost accounting at the time of the foundation of CIMA in 1919 and the subsequent development of management accounting and identifies current practices in management accounting.

Chapter 2 Costs: Modern, Future and Strategic
Strategic cost analysis with a focus particularly on multi-product costing, strategy and management accounting in investment decisions including synergy, portfolio effects and economies and diseconomies of scope. The economics of technological change on decisions and actions.

Chapter 3 Flexible Technologies, Fluid Organisations and Digitisation
Considers advances in a range of flexible organisational technologies and discusses the rise of 'fluid' organisations. It assesses the implications for risk and explores further certain strategy considerations and the widening boundaries of management accounting.

Chapter 4 Costs Co-creation and Globalisation
Assesses the changing nature of the product and the firm whereby the customer contributes to product development on a continuous basis and competitors can collaborate on some dimensions. Also covered is the added complexity of regulatory environments increasingly calling for standardised modes of compliance assurance and a discussion of issues relating to commonality of approach in measurement, valuation and financial representation.

Chapter 5 The Rising Tide of Change in Management Accounting
Explores aspects of the impact on management accounting of the global financial crisis beginning 2008, the sustained appeal to quantification in management

decision making and the structured logic of executive decisions and actions. These are concerns which in a world of extreme volatility and novel contingencies will be questioned and potentially lead to the reshaping of management accounting. The issue of collaborative alliances, virtual organisations as a special case of fluid structuring and other enterprise related effects provide a focus also for this chapter which concludes with a summary of important broad points made in the book.

The prognosis of the report is that management accounting has built a significant body of knowledge and of tested practices but that its potential for innovation and its capacity for regeneration can be expected to further burgeon. What is certain is that there is both an acceleration of uncertainty as well as growing uncertainty about volatility itself across enterprise environments today. As a consequence, assumptions, projections, prognostications and information analyses now take place with different expectations and objectives. It is incumbent on the management accountant to assess the propriety of continuing with the status quo. Now is the time to consider the pressures of factors which have arisen very recently including globalisation forces, the rise of virtual organisations and business models resting on digitisation, the more extensive regulatory climate facing organisations which influences norms of governance and transparency, and the engagement of greater risk analysis across a multitude of enterprise activities and endeavours. These factors and conditions are inherent elements of the new organisational order and will in the future influence management accounting discourse.

Chapter 1

Management Accounting: Past and Present

1.1 Introduction

Most techniques currently used in management accounting have distant origins. An understanding of their roots is useful in appreciating their deployment today. The first section of this chapter briefly investigates the development of cost accounting to the time of the founding in 1919 of the Institute of Cost and Works Accountants (ICWA) which evolved into the Institute of Cost and Management Accountants (ICMA, 1972) and in 1986 into CIMA. The chapter then tracks the development of cost accounting and management accounting from then to the present. Finally, the chapter considers the current state of management accounting and some of its practices.

There are different arguments for considering the past. One might suggest that management accounting has evolved and progressed over a historical time frame, essentially becoming more adept at confronting costing challenges. But such a view would presume the field's pursuit of betterment toward some ideal state and the existence of a pre-existing conceptual framework awaiting discovery. This is a problematic stance as management accounting would then seem to be capable of moving towards closure of some sort, for which no conclusive argument has ever been produced. A more viable approach is to understand the changes faced by management accounting and its response in the light of continuous change. This view proffers an understanding of the field's strategic posture under different circumstances. It permits assessments of its theoretical underpinnings as well as the practical changes it has undergone and which caused it to change. Such a perspective allows us to discuss technical and practical aspects of management accounting mechanisms from the vantage point of theoretical interests in their logic and structure. It also permits us to consider the field's reactions and potential changes as it faces an emerging future in the context of modern day globalisation effects, digitisation and technological advances, concerns with risk management, governance and sustainability and wider forces in evidence across markets, geographical borders and economic and social terrains.

1.2 Cost Accounting and Management Accounting: Then and Now

We do not intend to review the history of management accounting in great detail here; for this, see Edwards and Boyns (2006) and Fleischmann and Tyson (2006) which provide extensive descriptions of the early historical development of cost accounting in the UK and USA. These articles, and other research, indicate that much of this history is contestable because of sparse records and the continuing discovery of new sources of information. Many studies also suggest that market pressures and changes in management structures drove firms to develop certain specific internal accounting procedures (Chandler and Daems, 1979; Johnson, 1983). But there is evidence and arguments that accounting practices have much wider and more dissipated origins (Baxter and Chua, 2006; Bhimani, 1996; Hopwood and Miller, 1994; Miller and O'Leary, 1987).

1.2.1 Costing Then

The early history of accounting within the firm from the 1840s to approximately 1910 firstly involves predominantly bookkeeping for costs and for revenues, with a major purpose being the valuation of inventories for financial accounting purposes. Secondly, and secondarily, it involves the seeking of more sophisticated product costs and more accurately costed jobs, batches and orders. These developments tended to be the province not of accountants but engineers, and those accountants who were involved were financial accountants. Everyday costing was the province of a large army of unqualified clerks.

The most important accounting book on costing in the last quarter of the 19th century was an English book by Garcke and Fells, *Factory Accounts: Their Principles and Practice* (1887, with a large number of subsequent editions).[1] A good majority of their book addressed bookkeeping for costs and urged the integration of cost accounts with the financial accounting system, but their understanding of costs was surprisingly modern. For example, they discussed accounting for prime cost (labour and material) and accounting to provide accurate costs for pricing. They recognised the importance of the distinction between fixed costs and costs that are variable with output. They attributed those overheads to products that were believed to vary with production, including depreciation and supervisory costs but not fixed costs such as general administrative costs. This understanding of 'modern' fixed and variable costs supported early advocacy of the 'break-even' chart (Hess,

---

[1] Garcke was a working electrical engineer and company chairman. John Fells was a financial accountant who also worked in industry and became an adviser to many firms on keeping internal accounts.

1903). There is, however, little evidence that such costs were used for cost control or performance measurement.

These two strands – cost bookkeeping, including inventory valuation, and costing for pricing – later formed the core of cost accounting. However, these 'modern' views were not generally taken up by industry. Arbitrary rules of thumb for accounting, mainly for prime costs, predominated.

Concurrently with the introduction of new technologies, a variety of new methods of attaching overheads to prime costs emerged from around the 1880s, with the machine hour rate gaining acceptance between 1900 and 1910. This system had an impact on practice. The allocation of overheads, although general practice then as it is today, had its contemporary critics – this criticism mainly being that it is market prices rather than accounting numbers which matter in decision making, and that any allocation of overheads is arbitrary. Both of these criticisms are still believed by some to apply today, but practice overwhelmingly continues to use overhead allocation (Dugdale *et al.*, 2006) even though research consistently suggests that overhead allocation cannot be other than arbitrary (Thomas, 1969, 1974).

A conflict of views surrounds the causes of the birth of ICWA in 1919 and the effect of the First World War (1914–1918) on its founding and on costing more generally. One view is that the War produced forces and conditions which led to the professionalisation of expertise relating to costing practice. There existed strong backing and enforcement by the government for verifiable costing because prices had to be based on costs (Loft, 1990). The War thus sponsored the emergence of professionalised costing expertise. Other research, however, suggests that costing was practised widely across firms and industries prior to the War (Edwards and Boyns, 2006). This is not to deny that the War had a profound effect on the cost accounting profession. According to Loft (1990) the wide distribution of costing during the War and its continuing role in moderating inflation post-War created a suitable foundation for the formation of the ICWA[2] which she describes as the 'coming into the light of cost accounting'.

In the UK there was a wish among cost accountants to continue to enjoy the freedom gained from the dominance of financial accounting and auditing during the War. It was felt that the financial accounting bodies did little to encourage cost accounting and probably saw it as beneath the station of 'professional' accountants. The founders of the ICWA sought to make cost accounting fully professional, by providing education and examinations (not compulsory originally) and by seeking to make costing scientific. This was one of two objectives stated in CIMA's charter granted in 1976.

The scope of cost accounting around the time of the creation of ICWA is suggested by looking at the relatively few textbooks available at that time. One contemporary

---

[2] Originally titled the Institute of Cost Accountants Ltd but quickly changed to ICWA in order to avoid the Institute's designatory letters conflicting with the then Institute of Chartered Accountants.

American book is *Cost Accounting: Principles and Practice*, published in 1920 (Jordan and Harris, 1920). Their concern with the then lack of progress in cost accounting, and the promise they saw it offering contemporary American industry, is well expressed as follows:

> *Hardly any other feature of industrial procedure has been so necessary, yet so slow in developing, as cost accounting – so rich in possibilities of usefulness for management of business, yet so widely considered for many years as a doubtfully necessary evil. (p. iii)*

The book is largely concerned with the details of setting up a 'proper' cost system for each functional cost, thus purchasing and receiving goods were seen to require:

- records of transportation charges, stocks and material usage,
- the pricing of requisitions and
- the calculation of minimum and maximum quantities of orders.

Although at that time much of industry used rudimentary accounting systems rather than the leading edge systems suggested in the book, much of its content indicates early concerns with some of today's problems.

Cost accounting was then seen to concern not just pricing and inventory valuation but also cost control, but nevertheless this was in terms only of keeping accurate records, not generally in terms of comparison with plans. Standards are mentioned in the book, but only relative to the level of capacity usage that should be used when costs are to be estimated for pricing purposes.

Several chapters consider overhead allocation. They advocated department overhead rates using different rates within each department to try to capture the correlation between costs and activity usage, because of their believed greater accuracy relative to other methods. They also advocated the use of under- and over-absorption of overheads to deal with the variability of production, with non-recovered overheads being charged not to manufacturing cost (which was the general practice) but to the profit and loss account. Of course, from a research perspective at least, most of this would be regarded as irrelevant to decision making, control and performance measurement.

At the time of the foundation of what was to become CIMA, internal accounting focused on transactional accounting. The incorporation of mainline subjects, such as standard costs, budgetary control, performance measurement and costs for decision making, occurred subsequently within management accounting over a 90-year trajectory. The next section demonstrates this evolution by charting very briefly the development of cost accounting and management accounting from 1919 until the present time. Such a focus is important in understanding today's use of these techniques.

1.3 The Path to Today's Cost Accounting and Management Accounting

The pattern and timing of changes in cost accounting and management accounting from just after the First World War until the 1950s often seem to differ between the US and the UK (see Edwards and Boyns, 2006; Fleischmann and Tyson, 2006), with the US being the more experimental.

The first use of the title 'management accounting' seems to be by Robert Anthony in 1956 for the title of his American book *Management Accounting: text and cases* (Anthony, 1956; see also Horngren, 1962). Naturally, elements of management accounting were used earlier by some (mainly large) firms, and most of the techniques and methods which form the foundation of today's management accounting were in existence by the mid-1960s.

To illustrate the development of management accounting, the next sections look at the growth of three foundational elements of management accounting: standard costing, budgeting and capital budgeting.

1.3.1 Standard Costing

In the UK, fully-fledged systems of standard costing including variance analysis were first advocated in books from around the late 1920s, with some firms using such systems a little earlier. Publications on standard costing in the US appeared in the early years of the 20th century and it was quickly implemented by large firms, aided by the spread of scientific management techniques (see section 1.3.2 below).

1.3.2 Budgeting

The first UK text in the area of budgeting was published in 1931 (Willsmore, 1931), emphasising the need to compare plans with actual results. Around this time, a number of famous British companies such as Dunlop, Austin Motors, Cadbury and Pilkington Brothers practised budgeting. In the US, publications about business budgeting in the 1920s sought to transfer the well-established practice of budgeting in government to commercial organisations.

The advance of management accounting in the US was influenced by the ideas of 'scientific management' or 'Taylorism' – named after its leading proponent F.W. Taylor – which emerged in the 1880s and 1890s, with books appearing in the 1900s. The notion of standards for performance evaluation has more protracted origins (Hoskin and Macve, 1986; Miller and O'Leary, 1994). Taylorism saw manufacturing as being able to be objectively programmed and its efficiency optimised scientifically. Incentives and disincentives were given to workers to ensure the pursuit of standards of efficient performance.

After the Second World War (1939–1945), budgeting and standard costing were integrated but these methods probably did not become widespread in large- and medium-sized firms in the UK until the late 1950s or early 1960s. This, together with enhanced systems of managerial co-ordination and control, allowed the widespread use of responsibility accounting as we now know it. In 1954, a major study of seven major US firms (Simon *et al.*, 1954) suggested that their internal accounting systems contained and used most of the foundational elements of management accounting.

1.3.3 Capital Budgeting

In the first half of the 20th century, investment appraisal was based predominantly on variants of return on investment (ROI: earnings after depreciation/book value of investment) popularised by its use in Dupont. But payback was also important. One 1959 survey in the US indicated that over 90% of large firms used these methods with 66% using ROI-based methods (Istvan, 1961).

The use of the time value of money and risk analysis also has a long history in appraising investments in financial assets, and there is evidence of some usage of these methods for investment appraisal in the 1920s by industrial firms in both the UK and US. Indeed, there are much earlier isolated instances of its use by a few firms. Capital budgeting using the time value of money via discounted cash flow (DCF) methods, including net present value (NPV) and internal rate of return (IRR) criteria, was advocated extensively in the US in the 1950s (Anthony, 1956; Dean, 1951). Possibly, the most well-known American book was *The Capital Budgeting Decision* by Bierman and Smidt, published in 1960 (Bierman and Smidt, 1960). These books had ripple effects in the UK. The first UK book in this area, published in 1963 (Merrett and Sykes, 1963), was more theoretical than the American books. In both countries the take-up by large firms was some 60% by the 1970s, reached over 80% in the 1980s and is near 100% in the 2000s.

Generally, very few accountants made any contribution to capital budgeting theory, even though it was management accountants who 'owned' capital budgeting in practice and who had to solve the many practical problems of investment appraisal implementation. This lack of contribution by accountants to capital budgeting has continued, and finance researchers have recently been more focused on real options-based investment evaluation. This presents an opportunity for management accountants, both practitioners and researchers, to take the lead in the further development of capital budgeting (see Bhimani *et al.*, 2006, 2007a).

1.4   Other Research Thrusts

Research in the period 1950–1970 led to many other innovations. To give an idea of the opportunities available to practising management accountants at that time and how far management accounting has developed since then, we will look very briefly at a classic collection of research articles written in the 1960s entitled *Studies in Cost Analysis*, edited by David Solomons (Solomons, 1968). Many of the articles in the collection either considered new tools for accountants or introduced accounting researchers to new disciplines, such as operational research (OR). The new tools included linear programming, regression analysis and statistical control, elementary uncertainty and a mention of the theory of games. For management accounting practice today, the questions are about how far these new tools were adopted by industry, and whether they are now important in practice.

One perspective which seems to have had limited practical appeal was the possibility of integrating more OR with accounting. The aim was to invite accounting to use scientific modelling, especially linear programming and mathematical programming more generally, in an attempt to improve productivity by using certain decision models such as the adoption of forward-looking incremental costs under uncertainty. In contrast, accounting was seen as pursuing cost reduction using budgets and standard costs and lacking scientific models – a position that still prevails today. For a considerable time, linear programming and its variants featured in accounting research. However, the promise of this approach has been realised neither in research nor in practice, other than in the relatively few firms whose technologies make programming important, for example oil refining.

Research also looked at depreciation and found 'accounting depreciation' wanting. Instead variants of economic depreciation based on 'user cost' were suggested, that is the present value of the foregone alternative future use resulting from existing use, so depreciation would involve a comparison of economic rather accounting values. This approach is still not fully accepted today.

Ways of accounting for multiple products were suggested and the concept of attributable cost was advocated, that is the average cost per unit that could be avoided if a product or process were discontinued entirely without altering other aspects of the firm's cost architecture. The expansion of break-even analysis to allow for uncertainty and for the cost of capital (Jaedicke and Robichek, 1964; Manes, 1966) does not seem to have become more widespread later.

A number of other important research topics were also being considered around this time. Learning curves were explored at a very basic level (Bierman and Dyckman, 1971). This is a subject which is important in some industries, but generally has not been incorporated in cost functions used by accountants. The problems of accounting for joint cost and joint products were beginning to be raised, where jointness was reserved for joint products which generate multi-products in fixed proportions (Bierman and Dyckman, 1971). It was advocated that joint costs should be allocated using preferably the gross sales value method, but this is now seen as a deficient method (Bromwich and Hong, 2000).

Residual income (RI) was advocated by Solomons (1965) based on practice at General Electric in the US. RI is a performance measure based on accounting earnings less the firm's cost of capital on the book value of its capital. This performance measure later formed the foundations of the 'economic value-added' approach to maximising shareholder value – see Section 1.5.3 (Stern *et al.*, 1995). Another important theme of research at this time was the economic aspects of transfer pricing founded on the neo-classical economics paradigm (Gould, 1964; Hirschleifer, 1956, 1957). It was suggested that, in the simplest setting of a firm with two divisions (an intermediate product division and a distribution division), the transfer price between the two divisions should be set at the intermediate product division's marginal cost. A major paradox of transfer pricing, which still concerns later writers, was not however considered: firms exist to avoid market imperfections, but using economic transfer prices resurrects the – presumably – imperfect market within the firm. However, this area is not a current major research thrust and transfer pricing in multinational practice now seems more concerned with minimising tax and reducing the impact of regulation.

In summary, many management accounting techniques that are now used were in place by the mid-1970s following very rapid economic industrial growth in the 1960s and 1970s. For an alternative view, that internal accounting was fairly fully formed by around 1925 see Johnson and Kaplan (1987, p. 13). Figure 1.1 summarises the timing of the introduction of some important techniques in management accounting. The arrow pointing upwards to the right indicates that these techniques have been incrementally added to management accounting. The next section reviews some of the most important modern developments.

1.5 Management Accounting Now

1.5.1 Activity-based Costing (ABC)

The cost structures used in management accounting have changed very little since the early days of internal accounting and are very simple. Direct costs – such as materials and components, labour and machine time, and variable overheads – are treated

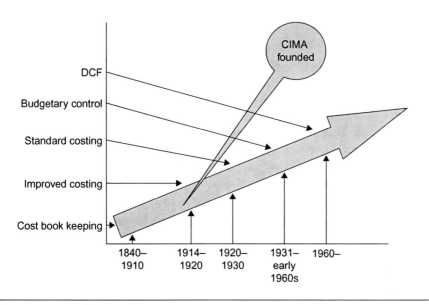

Figure 1.1 Evolution of Management Accounting.

as if they vary proportionately with product output. The assumed simple cost drivers used reflect the technologies of the firm in a 'broad-brush' way – labour hours for labour-intensive elements of the organisation and machine hours for capital-intensive sectors. With traditional overhead absorption methods, a two-stage process first attributes costs from resource pools to cost pools attached to manufacturing activities, using relatively sophisticated bases. In the second stage, these overheads are allocated from cost pools to products or other cost objects, usually using very simple volume-based overhead charge-out rates – thereby potentially distorting information. The use of volume bases thus takes fixed costs and converts them into seemingly volume-based costs.

ABC was originally introduced in the US in the late 1980s to remedy the distortions to product costs caused by this second stage allocation. ABC was refined from practical observations by Cooper and Kaplan (Cooper, 1987; Cooper and Kaplan, 1987) and strongly supported by the US defence industry. As is well known, ABC seeks to attribute overhead costs from overhead resource pools directly to cost pools, each comprising costs that are driven by a common and unique cost driver. Cost objects, such as products, are then charged for the activity units they consume from each cost pool. The essence of the difference between ABC and traditional allocation procedures is that the effect of cost pool activities on cost pool costs should ideally be traceable or measurable, and thus should be objective. That is either the relationship is known from the technology employed, so that each activity unit is known to require a given mix of inputs, or the inputs used can be measured to activities in the same way as utilities' consumption is measured (e.g. by using meters). In practice, often less rigorous methods are used, thereby raising the prospect of the re-entry of overhead allocation.

There is no doubt that in the late 1980s and early 1990s ABC was the subject of a major evangelical campaign, mainly by consultants, to urge its very widespread take-up. The activities' logic was also extended to management by activity and to budgeting (ABM and ABB respectively). Often extravagant claims were made with regard to what ABC could do and its possible scope across industries. The first book in this series – Bromwich and Bhimani (1989) – sought to give a more balanced account of the strengths and weaknesses of ABC and its variants, and questioned whether ABC should supplant traditional management accounting. There is evidence now that the current take-up of ABC runs at around 20% in larger firms in the UK and US, though some American studies suggests a deployment rate of around 40%, including those considering implementation (Bhimani *et al.*, 2007a; Innes *et al.*, 2000; Kianni and Sangeladji, 2003).

1.5.2 Balanced Scorecard (BSC)

The second major innovative concept – the Balanced Scorecard (BSC) – had applications extending well beyond accounting to management more generally. This was introduced by Kaplan and Norton (1992 and 1996) and, as with ABC, it resulted from refining and building on observations of practice. As is well known, the BSC reports a linked structure of four kinds of information that support the firm's strategy, much of which is not financial information. Financial reporting in the context of the BSC focuses on shareholder value. The other information groups are: customer satisfaction (diversification and product attributes); internal processes (including the integration of functional perspectives, reporting critical enterprise activities for customer satisfaction and core competences); and the firm's innovations (adaptation to external changes and improvements – the ability to learn and improve). The use of the BSC has moved over time from being a strategic performance system to a fully-fledged scorecard that helps implement the firm's strategy through communication, developing action plans and being a basis for incentives. These applications are mostly still at early stages. The BSC has also provided a new role for management accountants when in charge of consolidating the information in the BSC, thereby increasing their exposure to other organisational functions.

Although there has been much academic criticism of the BSC, its diffusion across large firms internationally has been extensive. With regard to the BSC, a study conducted by Bain & Company found that, out of 1,221 international firms, 66% reported using the BSC – a 9% increase in 2 years (Rigby, 2007, p. 14). The degree of diffusion is greater if we include both reporting systems invented independently by organisations and those that have been internally customised. And here the term 'organisations' is used because the BSC and its influences have strongly affected both the profit-focused and the non-profit sectors of the economy. There is, however, a lack of hard evidence that BSC use improves performance. Norreklit (2003) restricts her critique to arguing that the reason for its wide acceptance is the appeal of the seemingly compelling arguments constructed by its advocates. Another major concern is whether management has the ability to trade-off and prioritise information from the four categories. De Geuser *et al.* (2008) used a sample of mainly large international companies based in a number of European countries. They found that managers believed BSCs improved organisational performance, widely defined, mainly by allowing strategies to be converted into strategic objectives and then be monitored and evaluated regularly. As with many managerial innovations it may be difficult or impossible to quantify the benefits of the BSC in financial terms.

The BSC reports on how well the firm's strategy has been accomplished, that is strategy is assumed to be settled. CIMA (2007) introduced a 'strategic scorecard' to seek to help in the development of strategy (see Section 4.6). This firstly summarises the key aspects of the environment in which the organisation is working, so that senior management can be aware of changes in the external environment and alter their strategy in a dynamic and volatile environment. Its focus is thus on strategic change. Secondly, it identifies options that can be further developed and implemented. Thirdly, it sets milestones for the selected plans, and finally it highlights the risks associated with the organisation's strategy. The strategic scorecard thus reports on the organisation's strategic position, strategic options, strategic implementation and strategic risks. It is too early to evaluate the likely take-up of the strategic scorecard but it does appear to fill an information gap.

1.5.3   Value-added Management

The RI approach was revivified and commercialised as a share value maximisation model, initially by the consultancy firm Stern–Stewart in the mid-1990s. The underlying approach was invented in the 1930s (Preinreich, 1938) and, as was said earlier, was used by the American firm General Electric in the early 1950s (Solomons, 1965) (see Section 1.4). However, it did not gain much traction, perhaps because of the required need to abandon aspects of the then generally accepted accounting principles (GAAP). Stern and Stewart's approach is entitled Economic Value Added (EVA$^©$, which is copyrighted by them; Stern *et al.*, 1995).

1.5.3.1   Logic of Value-added Methods

EVA$^©$ is defined as GAAP earnings with some accounting adjustments less interest charged on the accounting book value of the firm's capital investment, again with adjustments. Thus, for example, research and development is capitalised. Interest is defined as the firm's cost of capital. The adjustments to accounting figures serve to make them more congruent with economic values without allowing anticipation of profits by valuing assets at their economic values. Other consultants have their own approaches with somewhat different emphases but here we will focus on EVA. The major reason for the adoption of these models is summarised by Cadbury Schweppes as follows:

> *Our objective is to maximise the value of Cadbury for our shareowners. An important financial tool that helps us measure value is economic profit. Traditional ways of measuring performance, such as operating profit after tax or earnings per share, do not take into account the full cost of the capital used to generate those profits. Capital is a combination of the funds provided by shareowners and money borrowed by Cadbury Schweppes, which we use to run the business and fund assets, such as property, office equipment, machinery and working capital. All capital has a cost which must be taken into account to calculate the economic profitability of our business. We only create value when we make a profit greater than the cost of capital invested.*

> *Cadbury Schweppes Glossary, 2008*

The objective is thus to seek to maximise shareholder market value by selecting investments that earn more than the firm's cost of capital. This is achieved by incentivising managers to seek out projects with positive NPVs. Such projects are those with a positive total of annual EVA's discounted for the year of receipt, so the present value of the sum of the discounted EVA's will equal the project's NPV. The essence of the argument is that managers can be either value creators, who increase market value relative to book value of assets at their disposal, or value destroyers by failing to generate a market value greater than book value. Ideally, the firm's net book value plus its discounted future accounting super-profits (EVA's), as seen by the equity holders, would equal equity market value. EVA is therefore seen as both an incentive mechanism and a monitoring device.

Shareholder value maximisation has in many ways swept the board in terms of adoption by large companies, especially major international firms. The list of international companies that use value-added methods, such as EVA, is long. Users of fully-fledged value-management approaches in the US include Coca-Cola, AT&T, Procter and Gamble, and Quaker Oats. In Europe they include Akzo Nobel, Boots, Daimler-Benz, Electrolux, Norsk Hydro, Unilever and Verba. Some adopters have, however, given up these methods. One reason suggested for this is that a single value-added measure cannot capture the full richness of a firm's performance as suggested by value-added proponents. Often the adoption of these methods follows periods of financial stress. There are, of course, a number of other reasons for the adoption of these methods but performance improvement and the need to align investment more to the core business are important, as is dissatisfaction with traditional performance measures (Jönsson, 2006, p. 119).

1.5.3.2 Problems with Value Management

There are a number of problems with EVA. To begin with the relation between a project's NPV and the discounted value of the project's annual EVA's applies to individual years only when a depreciation method based on annual cash flows relative to total project cash flows is used, which is unlikely to be captured by any possible accounting adjustments. The problem is that yearly EVA's may be negative and are not necessarily good indicators of that year's contribution to the project's NPV and it is therefore impossible to pay sensible bonuses on these. The extreme of the problem is illustrated by the Enron bonus scheme which paid a very substantial bonus to the originating executive based on project NPV immediately following the project being authorised, with obvious incentive problems.

Research has suggested that this type of model is the only model that will lead to maximising shareholder value, but only if depreciation amounts are based on yearly cash flows relative to the total cash flows generated by the project, that is years with the largest yearly cash flows bear the greater depreciation (Reichelstein, 2000; Rogerson, 1997). This is necessary as otherwise an annual EVA for a project is not necessarily consistent with the project's NPV. For example, the simple EVA in any year of a project may be negative or low even though the project has a positive NPV (Bromwich and Walker, 1998). This very different depreciation pattern to those generally used in accounting inhibits the approach's acceptance in practice, and it is not used by commercial value-added management models. Rather, either negative EVA's are not charged to the project until it achieves positive earnings, or annual bonuses are paid into a 'bonus bank' so substantial proportions of yearly bonuses are withheld and released in later years, thereby smoothing the effects of negative or low EVA's on incentives.

More generally, the accounting adjustments that seek to render accounting figures nearer to economic ones are only based on commonsense approaches, such as capitalising intangibles, and are thus, perforce, arbitrary. There is doubt whether the stock market uses EVA-type numbers to value companies rather than accounting earnings (Chen and Dodd, 2001). Another major concern is that EVA makes the generation of projects the predominant objective of the firm and thus may lead to the neglect of other managerial tasks, such as managing existing assets and the firm's workforce.

Given the above concerns, plus the current financial crisis with its origins in bankers gaming against complex bonus systems, it is likely the objective of maximising shareholder value may become more muted in companies, unless they can demonstrate that necessary and sufficient governance systems are in place. It is likely that corporate statements will refer more to the welfare of other stakeholders. Similarly, it is likely that value-management approaches will be less enthusiastically taken up by firms, and more effort will be made instead to overcome their problems. Moreover, in a financial crisis efforts to improve EVA's are likely to be directed towards reducing firms' capital bases (cost reduction) rather than searching for new projects.

1.5.4 Re-engineering the Finance Department

One of the major changes in management accounting in practice is the re-engineering, restructuring and downsizing of the finance function (see Asae, 1997). Much of this has become possible because of changes in computerised information systems and alterations in communication platforms. Almost all transaction accounting for instance is now processed by global or comprehensive information systems, including billing and collecting revenues, purchasing and bill payments, general accounting, payroll, tax filings and tax payments, accounting consolidation, cost bookkeeping and asset accounting. The use of information systems allows previously discrete systems across the firm to be consolidated into fewer systems which can themselves intercommunicate. They become seamlessly integrated across sub-units and indeed across autonomous firms. Thus, for example, BT has reduced its number of global information platforms from over 20 to 3. Prior to this type of consolidation exercise, different elements of the firm, each with a variety of different business models, different charts of accounts and different accounting systems operating under different regulatory models, produced information which had to be consolidated centrally. Operations to consolidate different accounting platforms can, for larger firms, take much time and require extensive resources.

These alterations in information exchange and collation have allowed many large firms to outsource their transaction accounting to countries which are cheaper and which possess a body of well-qualified accountants. All these factors have led to substantial headcount savings but have also, more importantly, freed management accountants for more analytical work and for different types of activity. They are less focused on more efficient information processing.

Re-engineered finance departments share a number of characteristics. These include accountant breaking out of the previous accounting 'silo' mentality so as to integrate with other functions and acting as team players within other functions. They can see other functions as customers for accounting services, and utilise high levels of technological controls to provide consistent data from fully integrated systems with single data capture which incorporates non-financial information. Of course, many re-engineering projects fail to achieve their objectives, and firms do not always capture the intended gains obtained from systems roll-out (see Hall *et al.*, 1994).

The general effect of attempts to transform the finance department can be summarised by looking at the responses of 900 CFOs worldwide in the IBM study *The Agile CFO* (Treadway *et al.*, 2005) where the time the CFOs said they spent on transaction activities had declined from 65% in 1999 to 47% in 2005 – and this was expected to decline to 34% in 2008. The time freed was partially used on additional control activities; the time they spent on these activities amounted to 20% in 1999 and 27% in 2005, and this level was expected to be sustained. The majority of freed time was spent on decision support and performance management, where the time spent was 15% in 1999 and 26% in 2005. This was expected to increase to 40% in 2008.

Figure 1.2 shows the introduction dates of the above techniques and an estimate of their current take-up.

1.5.5   Other Developments

Of course, many other accounting innovations have been suggested over the last few years. These include strategic management accounting (SMA) and 'beyond budgeting' (Hope and Fraser, 2003). The latter suggests the functions of budgets can be fulfilled in other ways and the problems attached to budgeting – such as being static, time-consuming and encouraging gaming by managers to get a better budget – can

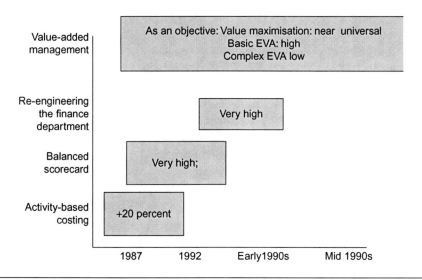

Figure 1.2   Penetration of New Methods in the UK.

thereby be avoided. Reviews of the firm's social responsibility operations and published strategic reviews (operating and financial reviews), in which management accountants could have a strong role, are also recent innovations. Similarly, many managerial innovations have impacted on management accounting, for example changes in performance measurement systems and enterprise resource management systems, such as SAP and Oracle (see Section 3.4).

1.6   Practice: Where We Stand Now

Surprisingly, there is a lack of comprehensive surveys on what firms actually do in management accounting, though there are many surveys looking at specific areas and some of these are referred to in this chapter. Here we review some recent, mainly UK, surveys to give a picture of the current state of management accounting, focusing on product pricing and emphasising how sustainable traditional accounting has proved to be. Survey findings at best reflect their sample which is often weak and not necessarily general. This needs to be borne in mind when interpreting the results stated below.

First, it can be said that firms do not generally use different accounting systems for financial and management accounting and these systems seem to reflect financial accounting requirements. However, the existence of flexible databases allows management accounting information to be customised from a single information system or single database. This is, of course, necessary to provide appropriate costs for decision making and control purposes (Brierley *et al.*, 2001, pp. 215–216).

Secondly, in manufacturing firms materials and components on average account for the greater proportion of manufacturing costs, followed by overheads, with labour cost being a small percentage. For example Al-Omiri and Drury (2007, p. 413), in a sample of 176 large UK firms, found that for manufacturing firms direct materials accounted on average for 52% of total manufacturing cost, whereas labour accounted for 11% and indirect manufacturing costs amounted to 10%, all with considerable variability. The relatively small proportion of indirect manufacturing costs may favour firms choosing simple costing systems. Looking at non-manufacturing firms they found that the percentages of direct costs relative to total costs were as follows: for financial and commercial enterprises 49%, for service enterprises 68% and for retail and others 66%, again with considerable variability. Their findings on the costing systems employed by firms seem fairly representative of UK large firms and suggest that firms are relatively conservative, though the substantial use of direct costing (variable costs) in their accounting systems does suggest that economic considerations are often taken into account. These findings are shown in Table 1.1.[3]

---

[3] The take-up of ABC may be overstated as the sample was skewed towards ABC users.

Table 1.1 Analysis of Costing Systems by Business Sectors

Business sector	ABC (%)	Absorption (%)	Direct costing (%)	No costing system (%)
Manufacturing	20	52	21	7
Financial and commercial	68	9	9	14
Retail and other	22	26	35	17
Service	33	17	28	22
Total (%)	29	35	23	13

Source: Adapted from Al-Omiri and Drury (2007).

With absorption costing, a large number of studies have found that direct labour overhead rates are used by 40–60% of the firms sampled. There is no doubt that this is still the predominant method of overhead recovery, with machine hours also being used or considered by firms with automated processes (see Brierley *et al.*, 2001, pp. 225–226). Another survey by Brierley *et al.* (2007) indicates that there are differences in usage of machine hours between different industries. Thus in the chemical products industry 50% of firms used the machine hour rate, whereas the rate for the industrial manufacturing industry was 42% and that in consumables manufacturing was 32% but, perhaps surprisingly, it was only 13% in electrical and electronic manufacturing. Not surprisingly Al-Omiri and Drury (2007) this study confirmed that ABC was not widely used; 29% of the sample used ABC or were open to its use, presumably with a favourable inclination.

There is evidence that firms use a variety of methods when pricing. For example, one study (Drury *et al.*, 1993) indicated that some 77% of firms often or always use full cost-plus pricing – though this is used selectively, with large firms especially allowing for the impact of demand – and 50% often or always using total variable costs in pricing. Larger firms are more likely to use this approach, and a substantial proportion used both methods.

The characteristics of practice in budgeting and standard costing have not been explored recently. Previous studies suggest that budgets are used in virtually all large manufacturing companies. As part of a study, Guilding *et al.* (1998)[4] obtained 303 responses from 260 UK firms in manufacturing, producing or processing with

---

[4] This study is a comparative one comparing UK and New Zealand practices. Only a few differences emerged, with New Zealand practices being more conservative.

an annual sales turnover of over £10 million. All the firms used budgets, suggesting that those who seek the abandonment of budgeting face an uphill task. Managers were held responsible only for costs controllable by the managers in 23% of the sample, whereas 52% of managers in their performance reports had both controllable and uncontrollable costs reported, albeit as separate entries. Total costs were reported in 23% of the responses. Flexible budgets were used in 42% of the sample. Variances against budget were regarded as of above average importance by 45% of the sample and of vital importance by 26%. This again shows substantial conservatism with regard to management accounting systems as it suggests that variances are used for control rather than learning for decisions.

The same study considered standard costing, with 76% of the sample using standard costs. Here respondents were asked about the methods used to determine standards, utilising a 1 to 5 scale where 1 means 'never' and 5 'always'. The mean scores for four methods imply that no one method dominated. The scores were really quite similar with the use of design/engineering being highest ranked (3.46), the use of work study and historical data being equally ranked (3.18 and 3.17) and standards based on observation being ranked fourth (3.06). Of the responses, 92% indicated that the level of difficulty of standards should either be 'achievable but difficult' (42%) or based on the average of past performance (50%).

Thus, budgeting and standard costing seem strongly supported but practised in a rather traditional way. A recent study of 41 UK manufacturing companies (Dugdale *et al.*, 2006) suggests that management accounting systems are basically traditional, featuring budgeting, standard costing and incentive systems based on accounting numbers. However, they report a strong emphasis on contribution reporting and reporting non-financial performance measures, which suggests some response to the changing environment.

The research literature generally surveying US management accounting seems to have experienced a lacuna since the 1980s. The most recent research article (Chow *et al.*, 1988) was a compilation of information from previous surveys. Their detailed findings suggest a similar position to that reported above for the UK, though the number of subjects dealt with is much larger.

There have been a number of US surveys by the accounting profession. The most recent survey of this type was by Ernst and Young/Institute Management Accountants (IMA) in 2003 which obtained nearly 2,000 responses from senior level executive members of the IMA in large and very large companies; some 40% were in manufacturing and some 16% in financial services/consulting (Ernst and Young, 2003). The percentage of direct material in manufacturing industries' cost was about 28%, labour was about 10% and overheads varied between 34% and 42%. Of the respondents 80% thought cost management was either important or very important to their organisation, and about 46% thought the demand for cost visibility was 'significantly greater' or 'much greater' than in the past. With regard to product costing, some 80% of the firms were using traditional costing and 70% were using overhead allocations. Interestingly, some 10% of firms had rejected these methods. Although no question was asked on the use of direct (variable) costing, its possible importance is indicated by the fact that about 60% of the firms used break-even analysis. Operational budgeting was used by some 76% of respondents and standard and activity-based, management-based budgets were used by about 62% of the firms. In performance measurement, some 62% of firms used benchmarking, 40% used BSCs and a little over 30% utilised value-based management. This survey, again, reveals a fairly traditional approach to management accounting.

1.7 Management Accountants as Business Partners

One global survey of 591 finance executives reveals that the largest group of respondents (43%) report that, in their organisations, the finance function serves as an integral part of the management team to support the creation of value by identifying opportunities and providing critical information and analysis for making enhanced operating and strategic decisions. This role was a more significant one to that of reporting and compliance (McKinsey, 2008). The survey revealed that 15% of firms surveyed saw the finance function's role as requiring a focus on reporting and compliance, with most time spent on transaction management in financial accounting. A slightly higher proportion (18%) saw its role as providing a focus on processes and risk minimisation, typically with key capabilities in management reporting, tax, audit and treasury. However, over one-fifth (22%) saw the finance function as playing a 'business partner' role, providing decision support to management via sound financial analysis for making financial and operational decisions. Respondents to the survey noted a marked increase from the onset of the global financial crisis in 2008 in chief financial officers' time spent on financial planning and analysis, financial risk management, strategic planning and credit decisions. Perhaps this will entirely dispel the 'bean counter' image of management accounting and recognise its morphing into a comprehensive business partnership liaison with management. Of especial significance is that the effort to reduce costs is expected to remain continuous and permanent.

The survey revealed very little increased centralisation of key tasks as a result of the global economic turmoil. Although the focus on certain activities has increased, the structuring of finance departments has not. In this light, 81% have reacted by focusing on reducing operating costs, 65% focus on cost reduction in performance reviews, 60% have reduced capital investments and 51% have heightened cash management.

The current economic crisis may be increasing the authority of accountants in firms. Until recently management has seen management accounting as only adding via the application of some techniques they most value. For example, Bain & Company undertakes regular surveys about popular management tools with a global sample of nearly 10,000 respondents (for details of the survey, see Rigby, 2007). This arranges 25 management tools in order of popularity as measured by usage. Benchmarking was the most used technique in their 2009 survey, with strategic techniques the next most important. Outsourcing and the BSC were ranked next, with downsizing being outside the top ten. No specific accounting techniques are in the top 25 techniques, though it might be expected that cost reductions will figure strongly in the next sample.

The broad trajectory of the management accounting changes discussed above suggests that both circumstantial as well as strategic and defined effects in the face of forces such as national cost concerns during the war, the rise of neo-classical economic underpinnings of financial decision making, the influence of the rhetoric of consultants and management accounting commentators, and the spread of competition from foreign markets among others have been significant. An important question today concerns the role of management accounting increasingly becoming a line function and business partner to managers, rather than its more conventional information support role. Major shifts are occurring today as globalisation unfolds, as the financial turmoil which began in 2008 makes its effects felt, as technological advances in digitisation and other domains spread and as ways in which managers act and react to information and their perceived need to effect change alter.

These ongoing transformations will continue to impact on the field, by altering its rationales and techniques and by reshaping perceptions of its most apt form and nature of input into the managerial function and as part of organisational processes. What remains certain is that management accounting is in a continuous state of change. Some changes will be strategic in terms of novel techniques and conceptual underpinnings and others will be reactionary and indeterminate, reflective of circumstances and opportunities. In many enterprises, management accounting is a function that will become less independent of operational and executive management functions. Emerging conditions and forces which are affecting the field are considered, in part, in the following chapter – which covers conceptual economic considerations – and in subsequent chapters, which bring to light the wider implications of the fast-changing managerial landscape which confronts the profession.

Chapter 2

Costs: Modern, Future and Strategic

2.1 Introduction

This chapter considers costs for decision making, technology as the foundation of the organisation's cost structure, costing in a multi-product setting and cost links to strategy. Many cost concepts are available for decision making and it is therefore easy to demarcate costs under different 'economic' conceptions. Indeed, many textbooks give narrow and sometimes even misleading prescriptions of the costs that should be utilised for decision making. Here, we set out the economic logic of costs for decision making. The chapter is technical in nature, resting on some economic argumentation. However, in subsequent chapters we extend our discussion to widen the significance of costs beyond a purely economic analytical base to bring to light alternative conceptualisations of modern-day complexities facing organisations.

Currently, management accounting generally makes very simple assumptions about cost structures, dichotomising costs into those that are directly variable with production and fixed costs which do not change with production, at least within capacity limits. This cost structure implies a very simple technology which ignores many other technological features, such as economies of scale. Modern and future costing, however, makes it important to look at the impact of more sophisticated technologies on costs. We will review Activity Based Costing (ABC) here as a way of introducing an understanding of some aspects of technology into management accounting.

Management accounting practice in many instances ignores the fact that many firms have large product portfolios produced in locations across the globe. This requires, in part, that modern costing considers the impact of economies of scope. Such economies arise where it is cheaper to produce a given portfolio of products together rather than to manufacture the same volume of each product separately. These savings are generated by economies in the shared resources of producing products together rather than separately. This is an example of costing problems that may be addressed using economic analysis.

Strategic management accounting (SMA) is a collection of techniques that attempts to make costs and other aspects of financial management more relevant to strategy and to strategic decision making. Cost and management accounting tend to be focused on the internal and historical costs of the firm, whereas strategy is future-orientated and looks outward from the firm to the market where the firm's competitors and customers are located. It is to be noted that the intertwining of strategy and accounting has distant roots which did not encompass specific concerns with future orientation and outward outlook (Hoskin *et al.*, 2006). From a modern formal perspective, aspects of SMA might be regarded as assisting in strategic pricing by taking into account competitors' prices, strategies and costs relative to the firm to determine the existing and future costs of the benefits provided by products to consumers. SMA also seeks to assist via target costing, which refers to ascertaining the cost of producing the bundle of benefits provided by a product and either reducing the product benefits or reducing the cost of providing the benefits in order to achieve the desired market price, and via costing both the firm's value chain and those of competitors in order to reconfigure the firm's value chain to achieve greater competitiveness. Specifically then SMA techniques seek to generate the costs of strategies rather than taking information from routine accounting reports.

It is clear that many enterprises practice aspects of SMA without defining it in such terms. Here, we argue that SMA in some contexts can benefit organisations. We believe that management accountants in some circumstances are well placed to develop and deploy SMA approaches, and in this regard SMA is part of the possible future of management accounting. But it is evident that present SMA conceptions need to be widened to take account of the extensive organisational complexities which are emergent. The next section looks at costs for decision making.

■ 2.2 Costs for Decision Making

Currently, with readily accessible computing resources and access to highly sophisticated cost information systems, it is easy to drown in cost information and to be inundated with a variety of financial information outlets and platforms. For instance, it is now almost facile to reconfigure spreadsheets so that they give information by different categories, for example geographical area, product ranges and cost types, and by other cost objects such as enterprise divisions, departments and cost and profit centres. It is equally easy mechanically to change overhead allocation bases, to 'flex' budgets, to change standards used in budgets and in standard costing and to conduct sensitivity analyses. Most advanced information systems allow users to 'drill down' to get more information on specific items, or indeed to aggregate and summarise detailed information.

The problem is that this abundance of information can be taken at face value. With regard to costs, this may mean cost information is used as if it were unambiguously 'fit for purpose' without the necessary understanding of the actual cost concepts used in compiling the information. Generally, spreadsheets and other financial reports do not make explicit the types of cost being reported. This lack of understanding is especially a danger with non-accounting managers using accounting spreadsheets. Accountants as 'business partners' can help here by producing spreadsheets that are customised to a manager's requirements, and by explaining the utility of different cost concepts for these requirements.

There are many different concepts of costs, each of which serve some purposes but may be incompatible with other uses. Below we consider which costs may be most useful for decision making and in what circumstances. Many pedagogical texts provide simplified examples. However, the cost concepts available for decision making are more subtle and nuanced than in current practice in management accounting. For instance, fully allocated costs generally distort decisions. Possibly the problems associated with using inappropriate costings for decision making are likely to be more severe in increasingly complex and volatile environments. These are the reasons why we revisit this topic. We use an economic perspective to examine the utilities of different types of cost. The essence of costs for decision making is that the cost concepts used should answer the question: 'what difference does the decision make to the firm?' We extend our discussion in subsequent chapters with an outlook that is wide and extends outside the reaches of economistic argumentation to achieve a realism that is more reflective of what organisations and managers face today.

2.2.1   Opportunity Costs

In economics, all costs are opportunity costs. The opportunity cost of an input is the net revenue forgone in its next best use (see Coase, 1938). In well-organised markets, the cost of using an input is its market price, as this is what must be forgone when the purchase is made. If an input is bought for a specific job, its opportunity cost is its market price. Similarly, if an input that is already owned were not used for a given job, the saving is its market price because in well-organised markets it could either be sold at this price or retained for future use, generating a saving equal to its price as its possession renders unnecessary a replacement purchase. Opportunity costs come into their own when the market price does not measure the value of the marginal unit of the input because of scarcity at this price. This situation is set out in Table 2.1 below, where input X is no longer available on the market but one unit of input X is possessed by the firm. The historical cost of X was £300. The decision for the firm is to choose one job from three, all of which require the unit of X.

Table 2.1 Opportunity Cost: An Example

	Job 1 (£)	Job 2 (£)	Job 3 (£)
Revenue excluding the cost of X	1,500	1,000	1,200
Costs other than for X	750	650	550
Profit excluding the cost of X	750	350	650
Opportunity Cost of X if used for:			
Job 1	650		
Job 2		750	
Job 3			750
Profit/(loss) net of opportunity cost of X	100	(400)	(100)

The historical cost of X is irrelevant to the decision as this amount is not realisable in the market and therefore is not a decision alternative for the firm. It also represents a 'sunk' cost, that is a cost that cannot be recovered by selling the unit of X in the market. If any job is taken, neither of the other two jobs can be undertaken. Thus X's opportunity cost is the largest forgone profit due to undertaking a job. For instance this is £750 and £350 if Job 1 and Job 2, respectively, are forgone by undertaking Job 3. Only Job 1 makes a profit when input X is valued at its opportunity cost for each job. Thus opportunity cost guides us to a potentially correct decision in a compact way resting on economic theory. It is important to realise that opportunity costs only yield signals to profit-maximising conduct if the decision problem is properly framed, that is all important decision options are included and correctly specified. This may be difficult as the realised profitability of rejected options will never be known.

Where no market price is available for resources, such as for intangible assets including research and development, the opportunity cost of their use has to be estimated. Indeed, this is one way of valuing such resources. The use of opportunity costs associated with existing decisions allows the allocation of elements of the decision to those areas of the firm working on the decision, for example by basing overhead charges on opportunity costs. Delegated elements of the decision may be altered provided that this does not change the foundation of the overall decision and thus maintains intact extent opportunity costs. Similarly, opportunity reasoning may allow the measurement of those costs within the firm that have no market value, such as the costs of resource congestion or depreciation with use imposed by the demands of managers on the rest of the firm.

In simple situations like that shown in Table 2.1, opportunity cost is strictly redundant. In our case, the profit-maximising decision could have been made by selecting that job which generated the most profit excluding the cost of X (row 3 in Table 2.1). In fact, it is generally the case that calculating opportunity cost is only possible when the optimal decision is known (Gould, 1962). However, this ignores the opportunity cost concept's contributions in forcing us to be forward-looking, to look at all options, to consider only incremental costs and to use a thought framework to guide us when considering complex projects. As opportunity costs are subjective and specific to the decision involved, they generally figure in *ad hoc* decisions and not in formal accounting systems. Thus their use may not be apparent from surveys of formal accounting systems. It is this subjectivity also which, when reflected in informal assessments, leads to political and behavioural consequences outside what might be expected within purely economic confines of decision making. It is also clear that decision making may rest on qualitative assessments of what could be quantified but which managers choose not to quantify and to treat qualitatively instead (Bhimani *et al.*, 2006).

2.2.2   Variable Costs

In accounting, variable costs are those which are either known or assumed to vary proportionately with unit output volume, that is if 1 unit of production requires 5 units of an input, then 10 units require 50 units and 100 units require 500 units. However, this proportionate relation with volume may differ between different inputs. It is a very narrow definition of variable costs, ruling out both economies and diseconomies of scale in production. It also allows no possibility of substitution between variable resources, that is, it is not possible to substitute one input for another. It does, however, allow different variable costs to be added together as it assumes that each type of cost is unaffected by either the level of or changes in all other cost categories.

Economics defines variable costs more generally (Chambers, 1988, pp. 49–81). Here it is required only that variable costs will be positive if output is greater than zero and that costs increase in total with volume – the total cost of a larger output will be greater than that of a smaller output. Thus the cost of a given variable resource associated with, say, 200 units of output will be larger than that associated with 100 units of output, but not necessarily in a proportional way. This allows both costs displaying non-constant returns to scale and batch costs to be considered as variable. ABC allows some fixed costs to be treated as variable with activity but not directly with production. Thus complex cost functions relative to output are allowed.

Variable costs are partly avoidable with a reduction in output or completely avoidable where output ceases. More costs become variable as the time period considered becomes longer and, thus, more costs become avoidable. Variable costs are, clearly, part of the cost of a decision.

2.2.3   Fixed Costs

These are costs that need to be incurred, usually prior to production, in discrete amounts for any production to be produced; they do not vary with output changes, at least within capacity limits. Fixed costs are, thus, non-avoidable if production is positive. With multi-products, fixed costs may either be associated with only one or with more products (product-specific fixed overheads) or with all products. No costs are fixed in the long run as this is defined as the setting when the amount of all resources can be varied[1]. Fixed costs may or may not figure in decisions depending on the circumstances. Clearly, fixed costs allocated on some production volume base should not be part of the costs of a decision. Such allocations are arbitrary, treating fixed costs as if they were variable and not representing the incremental costs of any decision. There is some evidence, however, that at least some fixed costs may be more 'sticky' than other costs, in that they may be difficult to adjust downwards – that is be escapable – with decreases in volume but they may be fully responsive to increases in volume (Anderson *et al.*, 1995). There is controversy over whether such stickiness arises from the nature of an asymmetric market adjustment process, where it is more difficult to sell spare resources than buy them, or from managers wishing to maintain capacity for the future (Anderson and Lanen, 2007).

2.2.4   Sunk Costs

Sunk costs are usually defined as those related to resources, the historical cost of which cannot be recouped either partially or fully in the market. They are the costs of resources that are committed for some period of time during which they cannot be avoided by the firm, but after which they become avoidable or escapable. The inability to release the firm from committed resources may arise because of legal commitments, the existence of inputs that are completely specialised to the firm's requirements, the presence of joint costs (costs of a resource which is available for use by more than one cost object) or input indivisibilities (where inputs, such as equipment or capacity, are available only in discrete sizes which may not

---

[1] Strictly, this requires an assumption of capacity that is perfectly adaptable to demand, otherwise the existence of resources that can only be bought in discrete sizes larger than that required for the level of production means that it is possible to have long run fixed costs (though these should be rare).

correspond to the desired level of output). Escapability may differ with the period in question and the possible causes of inescapability may only apply to some time periods. Generally, sunk costs do not enter into definition of costs that are seen as useful in decision making, but they are part of total cost and average total cost (TC and ATC respectively). There is however a wider view of sunk cost – that costs sunk in the market may still be recouped by other uses in the firm.

Often textbooks suggest that fixed overheads are not relevant in decision making because it is assumed that fixed costs are also sunk, but depending on their characteristics they may in fact *not* be sunk. Moreover, not all sunk costs may be fixed. It is possible that some variable costs may be sunk, as in the case of perishable goods. It is therefore incorrect to treat all fixed costs as sunk and therefore as inescapable.

For example, Baumol (1996, p. 57) says user depreciation – that is economic depreciation (the fall in value due to use), not accounting depreciation – is a fixed cost of using an aircraft on a route, but it is not a sunk cost as the aircraft could be assigned to another route. Strictly, whether the aircraft costs are sunk or not depends on the airline's aircraft capacity. If there is excess capacity, the aircraft costs are not chargeable to the route and are thus escapable for the route. Depreciation may not be sunk if the aircraft could be sold or leased out. Aircraft economic depreciation is chargeable and is a fixed cost if the airline has attained its optimum aircraft capacity. However, even here, it may not be sunk and may be escapable if the capacity on the route could be leased out. Where capacity is rationed, aircraft depreciation is fixed and again not sunk, if alternative usage within the airline is allowed. Here, the cost of aircraft usage is the profit foregone on the best alternative route (the opportunity cost).

2.2.5 Total Costs

Total costs are the sum of variable costs, ABC costs and fixed overheads. In practice, total costs will include allocated operating or manufacturing overheads and may incorporate fixed cost allocations from other parts of the organisation (divisional or central costs) – and they will include sunk costs. Neither total nor average product costs of this type are meaningful in a multi-product setting and generally they should not be used in decision making. The relevant costs here are those which are incremental to the firm because of the product's inclusion in the firm's product portfolio.

2.2.6 Joint Costs

Common costs can be defined as applying to 'a setting in which costs are defined as a single intermediate product or service used by two or more users' (Biddle and Steinberg, 1984). Such costs are really no different to conventional variable costs.

The common products or services used by elements of the firm can be traced to that element in the normal way.

Joint costs are the costs of resources which, once provided for the benefit of one product or part of the firm, are available also for use by other products at little or no extra cost. Such resources are not used up by the number of products using the resources. The extreme example, well known to accountants, is that of a joint product where a single input yields two or more outputs in fixed proportions; a lamb, for example, yields a fixed proportion of meat and wool. Joint costs in the context of a joint product 'apply to a setting in which production costs are a non-separable function of the outputs of two or more products' (Biddle and Steinberg, 1984, p. 4). The term a 'non-separable function' means that technology determines that two or more products must be produced in fixed proportion by the process. This is too restrictive a definition of joint costs. More generally, the essence of jointness in costs is that the resources underlying joint costs can be shared by cost objects with little or no cost. Again, this is technologically determined: once the process is actioned its output can be shared around the firm at little or no cost.

With joint products, accounting usually assumes in an arbitrary way that the relevant resources are required for the production of what is seen as the major product, such as meat in our two product case, and therefore the cost of the joint input is assigned to the 'main' product. The costs of the remaining 'subsidiary' products are those incurred for their production only after the split into multi-products. Alternatively, the costs of the inputs are allocated on some other basis, such as the relative revenues obtained from the joint products. These procedures are arbitrary, and where revenues are used any costs derived are not economic costs and cannot be used for pricing as they are based on revenue in the first place.

Examples of resources that manifest general jointness between cost objects are off-peak utility demands relative to peak demands, spare capacity, information technology, corporate advertising, corporate credit rankings and most intellectual property assets that are used widely once they have been set up. In utilities, investments are made to satisfy peak demands and therefore off-peak demands can be satisfied using the extant resources without charge other than any variable costs. Spare capacity can be used without cost assuming that the spare capacity cannot be sold or leased out. Information technology, like a database, once available can be used by other activities in the firm with little or no cost. Generally most information provision within the firm will possess elements of jointness.

Joint resources therefore provide what are called public inputs. Such an input is defined in economics as one which, when created for one or more uses, may be used for other purposes without major cost other than related variable costs. National defence provides an example, as does the policing of a local area. The attributes of a pure public input are very precise but many resources, such as the examples given above, have elements of these characteristics and therefore manifest a degree of jointness. A first attribute is that of simultaneous supply: when a resource is provided for one user it is also available to other users, for example an existing data bank. A second attribute of public inputs is that they can be used by multiple users without using up the resource, at least up to some constraint. Examples are provided by spare capacity or the use of public utility resources to meet off-peak demand. Three other attributes of public inputs are: non-exclusion by the supplier, the inability of users to opt out of supply and the inability of users to dispose of the input at no cost. These attributes do not necessarily apply fully to joint resources in firms – for instance the availability of information on a data bank may be restricted to those with the correct passwords. Firms do sometimes allow parts of the organisation to opt out of the supply of joint resources but this often seems to relate to relatively minor inputs, such as items of stationery. Almost all information provision will possess elements of jointness. As such generally intangible resources are of increasing importance within firms, this is a problem for accounting in both costing and valuing such resources. We will consider this later.

2.2.7   Incremental and Avoidable Costs

2.2.7.1   Incremental Cost

This is the usual way that economists look at the cost of adding a new product to the firm's portfolio or producing an increment to existing product volume. Incremental cost here is the additional cost to the organisation of producing a new product or additional product increment, given the firm's existing activities. This can be calculated by determining the firm's costs relating to both its existing activities and the new product or product increment and deducting the costs of the firm without the new activity to give the incremental cost of the new activity. Incremental cost (IC) can be written in symbols for, say, a new product as follows:

$$IC_i = C(y) - C(y_{n-i}) = C(y_i)$$

Where:

IC_i is the incremental cost of the new product i

n is the total number of products including product i

$C(y)$ is the total cost of the firm including product i

$C(y_{n-i})$ is the total cost of the firm excluding product i

IC_i thus measures the costs that the new activity imposes on the firm. It does not include the cost of resources shared with other products, nor any allocated costs.

Incremental costs are those that would be avoided if a new product or an increment of existing products were not manufactured without changing the supporting organisational structure (Shillinglaw, 1963). These costs are the variable costs of the increment being considered plus the overhead costs which are specific and exclusive to the increment or product (Sharkey, 1989, pp. 37–38). Incremental costs will depend on the time period considered. Where major or strategic decisions are involved this time period will be lengthy and will allow the replacement of assets, and alterations in resources and costs if necessary. The convention in such cases is to define incremental cost as long run incremental costs (LRICs). Currently, BT are required to use this approach in their regulatory accounts (BT, 2006). Where we are considering possible planned extra output, then the specific overheads relative to the increment will include overheads that will be sunk when incurred (Baumol, 1996, p. 58).

The justification for using incremental costing for decisions is that if revenue covers, at least, the incremental costs associated with the decision then the decision is sustainable over the long run. Closely related to incremental cost is avoidable cost.

2.2.7.2 Avoidable Cost

Here we calculate the cost that would be saved if the production of an existing product were to stop or a reduction were to be made to existing production. The avoidable cost of product that is currently produced is the total cost of the organisation, including the product under consideration, less the total cost of the organisation *without* the product. Using the earlier symbols, avoidable cost for cancelling a product can be written as follows:

$$AC_j = C(y) - C(y_{n-j}) = C(y_i)$$

Where:

AC_j is the avoidable cost of producing product j

$C(y)$ is the total cost of the firm with product j

$C(y_{n-j})$ is the total cost of the firm excluding product j

$C(y_j)$ is the avoidable cost of product j. Avoidable cost is equal to the variable costs of the product plus the product-specific overheads associated with the product, that is those that would be saved on cancellation.

The difference between incremental and avoidable costs is that incremental cost is forward-looking whereas avoidable cost looks backwards, in that it looks at changes in existing plans. Provided there is a well-organised market for inputs, the two concepts should give the same answers except where incremental costs include sunk product-specific costs. Below, we give an example of the use of avoidable costs which also examines the utility of some other cost concepts in a specific situation.

2.2.7.3   Example: Avoidable Costs

An airline is considering dropping one of its daily scheduled flights from London Heathrow (LHR) to J F Kennedy (JFK) airport, New York, using a Boeing 747 aircraft which returns the next day. The flight is one of four daily flights using Boeing 747s to New York scheduled by the airline. In order to help in its decision, the airline requires a report on the 'economic' cost of the LHR to JFK leg of the flight. The costs can be collected under the headings of the simplified passenger value chain below:

Stage 1	Stage 2
Ticketing, check-in and departure	Flight and disembark

The airline has provided selected information on the fully allocated costs of the flight which is shown in Table 2.2. The airline is aware that the information provided is neither comprehensive nor fully detailed, but would welcome guidance as to what part of this information they should use in their calculations. It is understood that assumptions will have to be made.

Here we have tried to estimate the avoidable cost of a scheduled flight from London to New York, where the cancellation is arranged with sufficient notice for the airline to make any possible adjustments; we often can only make suggestions about the relevance of the costs in particular cost categories. We understand that some of our suggestions and assumptions may be contested.

Stage 1: Ticketing, Check-In and Departure

Ticketing: If this is an allocated element of the cost of the airline's reservation system, these costs are not variable with the flight. If they are commission to travel agents then these charges are part of the firm's marketing operations. Strictly, this latter is an avoidable cost but only if the customers do not transfer to another flight of the airline.

Sales and promotion: These are not avoidable costs of the flight as sales and promotion activities are unlikely to be specific to the flight.

Check-in: If this operation is computerised then the allocated costs are not part of the avoidable cost of flight. If check-in is at a desk, this is a staff cost which is fixed and, therefore, not part of the flight's costs.

Table 2.2 Costs for Decision Making

Fully allocated cost of flying Boeing 747 on the LHR – JFK route (one way)

Aircraft navigation charges	£1,611	Rentals Generally basic aircraft are leased and the airline picks up all other costs of the aircraft	£3,683	Flight deck crew All costs that can be traced to pilots including training	£3,811
LHR airport charges	£1,751				
Flight insurance	£1,606	Flight equipment depreciation Written off over 20 years	£3,425	LHR – Station costs Costs while on ground	£5,297
Fuels and oil	£9,175				
Maintenance	£620	Cabin attendants	£4,267	JFK charges Station costs	£5,500
		Catering	£3,500		
Check in	£3,175	Ticketing	£1,000	Airport charges and landing fees	£2,200
General and administration Share of general overheads	£7,857	Sales and promotion	£9,261	Total cost	£67,739

LHR airport charges: Presumably related to the flight and therefore part of the avoidable cost of the flight.

Station costs: This is a cost attached to the aircraft and its logistics, not to a specific flight. This cost would have to be paid whichever flight or whichever aircraft was used.

Stage 2: Flight and Disembark

1. *Flight*

   Flight deck crew: Aircraft crew are usually paid a salary for what are called 'block' hours. Their cost is, therefore, fixed and not relevant to the flight as this cost is unchanged by the flight. The cost is not sunk as the crew can be used on other flights. More generally, where the airline has excess crew relative to its flights then using the crew on this flight has no cost. Where crew resources and flight demands for crews are in balance then using the crew on this flight has no economic cost. It is part of block hours. Crew costs would be relevant if pilots were scarce over the airline as a whole. In this case, the crew may have to be paid a premium for taking this flight, and this is a cost of the flight. An opportunity cost would have to be calculated if crew scarcity meant that another flight would have to be cancelled if this flight went ahead.

   Aircraft navigation charges: Presumably these are incurred only because of the flight and therefore they are an avoidable cost of the flight.

   Fuel and oil: The actual usage of these inputs is part of the avoidable cost of the flight. This cost should not include any safety fuel reserves.

2. *Aircraft*

   Rental of basic aircraft: This cost is fixed relative to the flight unless the availability of aircraft is constrained across the airline. In this case, the charge would be the opportunity cost of the use of this aircraft for the flight (the net revenue from the next most profitable flight).

   Depreciation of airline investment in aircraft: This is not a cost of the flight on a number of grounds. Here, depreciation is an allocated accounting cost and therefore does not reflect depreciation due to use of the aircraft on the flight, which could be relevant.

   Maintenance: Assuming that this is an allocated part of the general maintenance of a Boeing 747, this cost is not variable with the flight. Maintenance and inspection costs relevant specifically to the flight, if known, might be non-avoidable. However, even here it would not be part of avoidable cost if engineers were employed on a 'block' basis.

   Cabin crew: The argument concerning the costs of the flight deck crew applies here and, therefore, the cost is not variable with the flight.

Catering: The costs of the catering and drinks estimated to be used on the flight could be seen as a variable cost of the flight. However, catering meal orders to suppliers are made in bulk with a long lag before usage. In this case, the cost of the meals on the flight may be seen as a fixed cost of the flight as the relevant meals already exist and therefore will not be saved if the flight does not take place. Moreover, strictly the higher quality meals and drinks for business class and first-class passengers can be seen as part of a marketing strategy and therefore should not be charged to the flight.

Flight insurance: This would be relevant only if an extra payment had to be made for this flight. It is likely that insurance is arranged as a lump sum covering the usual activities of the airline.

3. *Disembarking at JFK*

   JFK airport charges and landing fees: These are presumably airport charges and landing fees that are variable with the flight, so they are included in avoidable costs.

   Station costs: If the flight were cancelled, these costs may not have to be paid. However, it is unlikely that the right to the landing slot would be cancelled without making a decision no longer to schedule the flight on a regular basis, and therefore this cost is not relevant to the flight.

   General and administration overheads: These are an allocated proportion of general overheads. These are therefore fixed; they do not change with the flight and are arbitrary.

   Conclusions: The suggested costs based on including only avoidable costs are shown in Table 2.3.

Table 2.3 Avoidable Costs for Decision Making

Stage 1	£
Possible travel agents' commission	Unknown
LHR airport charges	1,751
Stage 2	
Aircraft navigation charges	1,611
Fuel and oil	9,175
JFK airport charges and landing fees	2,200
Total	14,737

This example shows that using the economic costs of a decision may generate a result that is substantially different to that produced using the fully allocated costs assigned to the decision. The relatively low avoidable cost of the flight is not surprising as cancelling a specific flight on a specific day is a decision where very few elements of the decision are variable with the cancellation. Thus few costs are affected by the cancellation decision.

Moving up the decision hierarchy of operating flights to JFK airport allows more resources to become variable. Thus if the decision to cancel the flight were made permanent, this may allow marginal alterations to the aircraft stock and in the number of the flight and cabin crews. Similarly, adjustments may be made to the airline's insurance policy and to its catering orders. Finally, the aircraft may be able to give up its landing slot at JFK airport but is unlikely to make similar savings at LHR. Moving further up the decision hierarchy by cancelling permanently more of the daily scheduled flights would produce more savings. Finally, giving up the route entirely would produce savings in costs, such as check-in at JFK and terminal and lounge costs that do not figure in our calculations.

■ 2.3   Management Accounting and Technology

2.3.1   Introduction

Technology – here defined as the processes employed in producing outputs of goods and services – is an important determinant of costs and therefore of the value generated by goods and services. However, the educational and professional training of management accountants generally takes a very simplistic view of technology. For example, a paper entitled *The Roles and Domain of the Professional Accountant in Business*[2], issued by the International Federation of Accountants (IFAC), does not include an understanding of technology in its list of required capabilities of accountants working in business (IFAC, 2005, p. 4). In contrast, the original exam syllabus of the Institute of Cost and Works Accountant (ICWA) issued in 1919, as might be expected given the Institute's name, included elementary mechanical knowledge, workshop knowledge and – in the final exam – mechanical knowledge, including the relations between costs and design (Loft, 1990, p. 35). Of course, there have been many pleas for management accountants to understand technology, and a perennial complaint about management accountants in many organisations is their lack of technological knowledge. This is a major challenge to management accountants if they are both to be fully accepted as 'business partners' and to reflect dynamic technology correctly in organisational cost structures. This section

---

[2] This is their term for management accountants.

therefore sets out the role of technology in determining costs, and examines the possible need to embrace more sophisticated cost structures that reflect more complex technology.

2.3.2 Technology and Costs

The cost function or cost structure of a firm shows how costs vary with output. It is a function of the quantity of inputs used, which itself is a function of product volume and input prices. Cost is determined by both the technologies available for production and the relative prices of the inputs. The technologies available are really the recipes available to the firm to produce its output. Minimising costs requires the selection of the optimal technology given the relative prices of the inputs utilised. The objective is to use the cost function to minimise cost, subject to the constraints imposed by technology. Thus if we wish to understand cost behaviour and cost drivers, it is necessary to understand the relevant technology. The role of technology in determining costs can be clarified by considering the choice of technologies, which takes place in two steps (Chambers, 1988, pp. 8–18).

The area labelled ABC in Figure 2.1 shows all the recipes available for producing a given quantity of output by varying the two inputs available (material and labour). Any combination of the two inputs shown in the area ABC can be used to produce the given volume of output of, say, 100 units. A positive quantity of both inputs is required for any production. Combinations outside ABC are unavailable with existing technology.

The first step in finding the cost-minimising technology for a given volume of output is to determine the most efficient bundles of the two inputs for producing the desired output. The optimising process is shown in Figure 2.1. The line AB charts the most efficient outputs (the efficient frontier). Point a on the line AB shows the minimum amount of labour that needs to be added to a given amount of material to produce the desired level of output. Adding extra units of labour (moving rightwards from point a) is wasted as the extra units do not change the level of output if

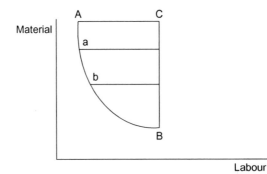

Figure 2.1 Technical Recipes.

the amount of material is held constant. Similarly, the amount of material at point a is the minimum which is required to obtain the desired level of output with the given amount of labour. All recipes not on line AB are inefficient, in the sense that they are dominated by the less input-intensive recipes on line AB.

Each point on the line AB, such as point a and point b, therefore represents an efficient recipe for producing the desired output. The slope of the line AB shows the amount of one input which must be added to compensate for a given reduction in the amount of the other input if the desired level of output is to be maintained. In economics, it is generally assumed that there are diminishing returns as one input is substituted for another.

This shows that to construct an accurate cost function, knowledge of technical recipes or technology in some detail is required. Of course, in practice, neither managers nor accountants may have the exhaustive knowledge of the issues assumed here. However, they should have such knowledge in their areas of normal operation. If not, they have to discover it.

Step two in finding the cost-minimising technology requires the choice of one optimal technology out of the bundle available. This is shown in Figure 2.2.

The selection from the available technologies depends solely on the relative prices of the inputs (Varian, 2006). Lines like P_1P_1 indicate the input mixes that have the same constant total input cost for a given output with different specific input prices, and therefore they can be called budget (or more technically, isocost) lines. Lines like P_1P_1 and P_2P_2 indicate constant output cost with different prices. The slope of the line P_1P_1 reflects the relative prices of the two inputs; here the price of material per unit is cheaper than that of labour. This line thus reflects the

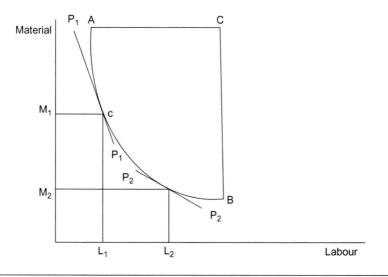

Figure 2.2   Demand for Inputs.

rate of possible substitution between the two inputs whilst maintaining the total cost of the two inputs. The line P_2P_2 reflects more equal prices between the two inputs.

The line P_1P_1, which reflects the rate of exchange between the two inputs, is tangential at point c to the line AB that connects all the efficient bundles of inputs. Point c thus indicates the efficient input bundle that minimises costs at the input prices reflected by P_1P_1. Reading across the two axes indicates that labour and material gives the demand for material and labour for the given amount of volume of output; M_1 and L_1 respectively. The total cost of the bundle of inputs shown by point c is $p_mM_1 + p_lL_1$, where p_l and p_m are the prices of labour and material respectively. This yields one point on the cost function for the output in mind, 100 units in our case. The full cost function with the same prices can be determined by undertaking this exercise for all possible volumes of output. The different demands for inputs with different relative prices using recipes from a given technology that are available for a given volume of output indicate how technological choices depend on changes in factor prices. Allowing input prices to change over the whole cost function charts the different demands for factors with changes in input prices. Thus demands for inputs are determined solely by the empirical properties of the cost function (Chambers, 1988, p. 57). For all the above reasons, it is essential for management accountants to do more to understand the firm's cost function by working in co-operation with technical and engineering colleagues.

2.3.3 The Accounting View of Technology and of the Cost Function

Currently, accountants entertain a very simple view of technology (Bromwich and Hong, 1999; Noreen, 1991). Implicit in their view is a technology which is unlikely to reflect that employed by modern firms. This technology is portrayed in Figure 2.3.

The available technology is shown by the area AOB. With the assumed technology, each unit of output requires so many units of material, say five, and so many units of labour, say three, in fixed proportions. This mixture of the two inputs is the only one that can be used. A lack of one input cannot be overcome by using more of the other input. No production is possible if either input is unavailable in the required amounts. Higher volumes of output simply require a larger bundle of the inputs to be used in the same fixed proportions. Thus both costs and technology are linear.

The above assumptions lead to there being only one efficient recipe in Figure 2.3 for the assumed volume. This recipe uses M_1 units of material and L_1 units of labour to produce our assumed 100 units of output, as shown by point O. With the assumptions, each unit of production requires $100/M_1$ units of material and $100/L_1$ units of labour. Thus this technology allows no substitution between material and labour – adding more units of either input just wastes the inputs. The total cost

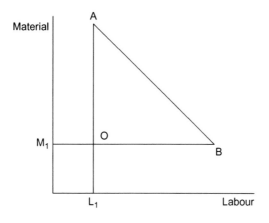

Figure 2.3   Technological Assumptions of Accounting.

of the inputs is given by multiplying the quantity of each input by its price and adding these costs together. With a technology involving multi-inputs, it is implicit that there is no jointness between the inputs. This means that the technological relationship between any two inputs is not affected by how much of a third input is used. The assumed technology therefore cannot capture the intricacies of modern cost functions. It rules out the possibilities of economies/diseconomies of scale and scope, and that resources may be used jointly by a number of cost objects.

2.3.3.1   ABC

It is not intended here to review the workings of ABC systems. These are well known and well handled in the text books. Nor is it intended to review the degree of usage in practice further than was done in Chapter 1 (a very good review of the studies of this and ABC generally is Gosselin, 2006). Here we look briefly at the assumed technology of ABC and consider whether this helps to explain its restrictive use. ABC represents an attempt to understand the technology underlying some fixed overheads by relating that technology to activities rather than product volume. Ideally with ABC the assumed relation between the inputs should be empirically validated, but often the application of these assumptions is just a matter of belief. The accounting technology described above is also used by ABC. Thus, it is assumed that the relationship between inputs is fixed and is just scaled up for volume of activity. Just as above we assumed a single product, a single and unique cost driver for cost pools is assumed in ABC. It is also assumed that activities in cost pools do not affect other cost pools. This assumption was implicit in the above analysis, where it was assumed that our product was isolated from all other activities of the firm. In a multi-input situation, there is assumed to be no jointness between the inputs used in a cost pool. These assumptions, together with fixed input prices, yield the familiar linear relationship between cost pool activity volumes and cost pool cost (Noreen, 1991). Cost pools cannot contain fixed costs as the assumptions of ABC assume that all inputs are fully variable.

These assumptions limit the possible application of ABC in practice. Many overheads do not behave in the assumed way. Thus while ABC and its variants are useful additions to the management accountant's toolbox they are not a general panacea for all accounting problems. One possible explanation for the poor take-up perceived to be shown in empirical studies is that different industries may face different levels of overheads that conform with the assumptions of ABC and, of course, different intensities of overheads in costs. Al-Omiri and Drury (2007) suggest this may be the case when they found that 68% of the financial services firms in their sample used ABC whereas only 20% of manufacturing firms did so.

Recent research has suggested that practical ABC costing systems can be made more efficient by seeking to improve the firm's cost architecture (see Datar and Gupta, 1994; Labro and Vanhoucke, 2007). This architecture comprises resource pools, cost pools and the number of pools entertained, the type of driver used for each pool and the precision of the measurement of each resource usage and cost driver (measurement error). Each of the above choices changes the structure of the costing system and alters the likelihood of errors and the types of error that can be expected.

Datar and Gupta (1994) for research purposes assume that the ideal cost structure is known, then derive variances from this ideal. Looking solely at cost pools and the products serviced therein, there are three possible types of product cost variance that cause the total costs of products to vary from their costs under the ideal system.

- A specification variance is generated because the cost drivers used differ from those used in the ideal system, assuming that the ideal number of cost pools is used.
- An aggregation variance arises where the number of cost pools employed is different to that under the ideal system.
- A measurement variance is generated where a less precise measurement of cost driver usage than is ideal is used in practice[3].

Generally we would expect that more refined systems with more correct specifications and more cost pools will produce better results, even in the absence of knowledge of the ideal costing system. This is generally confirmed by Labro and Vanhoucke (2007), who simulate a large number of costing systems. Management, although without access to the ideal, will have ideas as to how the cost system may

---

[3] More technically: specification variance=ideal product cost–product cost with ideal number of cost pools and known cost pool costs allocated using actual cost drivers for each cost pool. Aggregation Variance=Product cost with ideal number of cost pools–actual product cost.

be improved. Calculating variances using this system relative to using the benchmark existing system may provide indications of whether the revised system is a better approximation to the ideal than the existing system. Where the input mix in a cost pool is fixed, it does not matter which of the inputs is used as the cost driver. Any input, or driver correlated with an input, may be used as the cost driver for the pool in this case. Similarly, cost pools that have the same proportional input mix can be combined.

But proceeding by trial and error may make things worse. First, it is possible that difficulties in measuring correctly the cost driver usage by products will give rise to measurement errors. The likelihood of such errors increases with refinement of the accounting architecture. Thus with increased refinement, the measurement variance may offset improvements in the specification and aggregation variances (see Datar and Gupta, 1994). Secondly, Datar and Gupta (1994) show that seeking to improve some cost pools in a poor system may make things worse as previously variances may have been offsetting and refining part of the system, increases the total variance from the benchmark system. Thus, the general guidance is to continue to refine systems unless the improved variances generated by refinements are negatively correlated with other known errors.

2.3.4   Economies and Diseconomies of Scale and Scope

Economies of *scale* are generated when increasing production volume allows a new technology to be used that reduces the amount of variable resources needed to produce a unit of production, and therefore reduces the cost of a unit of product. An example would be where there is a minimum level of volume that needs to be reached before operations become efficient. Diseconomies of scale arise where there is some inhibition on production, such as the scarcity of an input (including capital assets – constraint on land is the usual example). Constant returns mean that no economies or diseconomies of scale emerge with increases in scale (Varian, 2006; Chambers, 1988, pp. 22–25). A constant returns assumption is employed by both the accountant's assumed technology and by ABC. With constant returns, production can be carried out in replicated plants of any size. Increasing returns (economies of scale) favour the centralisation of production in one facility while decreasing returns (diseconomies of scale) indicate that smaller plants would be more efficient. The accountant's assumed technology rules out both increasing and decreasing returns; the possibilities of economies and diseconomies of scale are ignored by most accounting textbooks and by much professional training. It is important therefore for accountants to consider the results of recognising that most firms are multi-product or multi-service with multi-locations across the globe.

Dealing with firms with large product portfolios produced in locations across the globe also requires that modern costing considers the impact of economies and diseconomies of *scope*. Such economies arise where it is cheaper to produce a given portfolio of products together rather than to manufacture them separately. Diseconomies of scope arise where it is cheaper to centralise production of individual products or similar products in customised, single, focused and independent production units (Sharkey, 1989, pp. 62–72). The advantages of economies of scope may be dominated by economics of scale and *vice versa*. Economies and diseconomies of scope provide an example of costing problems that need to be solved in order to generate better future management accounting. Another accounting problem is costing shared or joint resources, as these resources are difficult to 'cost' in an economically sensible way. This is made more difficult because many of these costs are generated by intangible resources, which themselves are problematic for accounting. The valuation of such resources and the costing of their use are still open to debate.

2.3.5 Economies of Scale

The first problem in adapting our usual cost procedures for the presence of multi-products is to define multi-product economies of scale. This analysis also helps to understand multi-service enterprises. Generally it is impossible to aggregate heterogeneous products in any meaningful way so we adopt an alternative approach (Baumol *et al.*, 1988, pp. 57–58). This is to select arbitrarily a given bundle of products made up of a fixed proportion of products and then to observe its costs as we increase the number of bundles produced. Such a given bundle of products is shown in Figure 2.4.

The horizontal axis shows the volume of multi-product output, that is the number of bundles of the assumed mix of products produced, and the vertical axis plots total cost. Figure 2.4 shows that, with multi-product economies of scale, total costs increase with output but at a decreasing rate. The unit cost of a bundle decreases with the number of bundles.

In this situation, average cost applies not to individual products – a misleading and dangerous concept in a multi-product situation as it can only be generated using arbitrary allocation. Rather, with multi-products average cost is defined as the total cost for a given volume of product bundles divided by the number of bundles produced. With increasing returns, average cost decreases with the number of bundles. Multi-product economies of scale are defined as occurring where the total cost of a given volume of output bundles is greater than the cost of the given volume evaluated at the variable cost (strictly the marginal cost) of the marginal bundle. This indicates the overall economies of scale associated with production. Such economies of scale are the result of product-specific economies of scale.

The costs of a product within a bundle can be determined by calculating the average incremental cost of the product (see Section 2.2.7.1 above, and Baumol *et al.*,

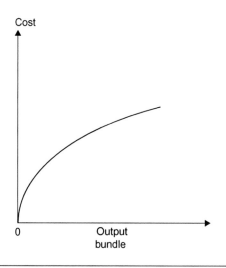

Figure 2.4   Multi-Product Economies of Scale.

1988, pp. 68–70). Here we vary only one of the outputs in a bundle and see how costs change. Thus the incremental cost of product I (IC_I) at a given volume of bundles is the total cost of producing the bundles including the costs of product I minus total costs without product I – the saving from not producing product I. Dividing the total incremental cost of product I by the volume of the product yields the product's average incremental cost (AIC_I). This is the average cost that is avoided when the product is not produced while maintaining the rest of the bundle intact. A product should only be in the bundle if the revenues it generates at least equal its incremental cost. Product-specific economies of scale are present when a product's average incremental cost is greater than its variable (marginal) cost at that volume (Baumol *et al.*, 1988, p. 68).

   Such economies arise where it is cheaper to produce a given portfolio of products together in one plant rather than to manufacture the same volume of each product in separate stand-alone facilities using the same technology (Baumol *et al.*, 1988, pp. 75–83). Such economies of scale arise because products are able to share resources, all of which would have been necessary for each product if each had been produced in separate facilities. It is such economies that justify the existence of multi-product firms. Similarly, diseconomies of scale favour firms that focusing on one product only, or on a set of similar products.

2.3.6   Economies of Scope

The most familiar example of economies of scope is, perhaps, the existence of joint products where it must be cheaper to produce together beef and hides in a single firm than in two specialised firms, which would involve wasting one of the joint products. More generally, economies of scope are generated by the many resources that have the characteristic that, once provided, they can be shared by cost objects at little or no incremental cost (see Section 2.3.7 below) whereas otherwise they would have to be provided for each product separately. In utilities investment is determined by the anticipated peak demand, and the capacity provided can be used to meet off-peak demands with a very small incremental cost. Other situations where economies of scope may arise are:

- where inventories can be shared between products, thereby reducing the level of stock that needs to be carried,
- where there is sharing of indivisible assets between products,
- where software and data banks exist which can be made generally available in the organisation or in parts of the organisation,
- where there are corporate items such as advertising and financing.

Figure 2.5 indicates the effects of economies of scope on total cost.

Cost is shown on the vertical axes. The horizontal axis shows the possible mixes of the two products as the proportions of an arbitrary bundle of a maximum of either 100 units of Product 1 or 150 units of Product 2 are altered, from producing 150 units (100%) of Product 2 and zero units (0%) of Product 1 – at the left of the Figure – to 50 units (50%) of Product 1 and 75 units (50%) of Product 2 – mid-point, to producing 100 units (100%) of Product 1 and zero units (0%) of Product 2, at the right of the figure.

The cost axis on the extreme left of Figure 2.5 shows the total cost if all resources are devoted to making only Product 2. In the presence of economies of scope, the figure shows that increasing the proportion of Product 1 from zero with a matching proportional reduction in Product 2 reduces the total cost with the minimum total cost being where there is a product mix of 50% of both products (50 units of Product 1 and 75 units of Product 2). Moving rightwards from this point indicates that total cost rises as the percentage of Product 1 increases up to 100%. With our example, for economies of scope to dominate multi-product economies of scale the total cost of producing the optimal volume (50 units of Product 1 and 75 units of Product 2) must be lower than the aggregate cost of generating the same quantities of the two products in two separate dedicated facilities, assuming the full advantage of the economies of scale from producing 100 units of Product 1 and 150 units of Product 2 respectively, which is the level of production that offers the maximum advantage of any possible economies of scale (Baumol *et al.*, 1988, pp. 82–85). Obviously, this condition may not be met for all volumes that the firm might produce.

This may all seem rather complex. However, the lesson for management accountants is clear – the possibilities of economies of scale and scope and their

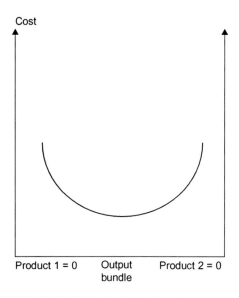

Figure 2.5 Economies of Scope.

relationships need to be considered in major strategic decisions, including substantial outsourcing decisions. Following the traditional accounting view of cost generates incorrect decisions that do not take into account all the possibilities associated with such decisions. However, the presence of economies means that costs at any volume have to be estimated as precisely as possible, and the ease of dealing with costs that are linear with volume is lost. Such estimates are statistically difficult to derive and are often contestable because of the methods used.

It is not really possible to review here the empirical evidence on multi-product economies of scope. However the theory suggests that economies of scope are one factor that encourages diversification, and economies of scale similarly encourage large, focused firms. There is a large number of studies that look at specific industries in relation to this, with a variety of results.[4] Generally the evidence supports the idea of constant returns to scale, at least in the range of volume in which firms operate, but with some findings that economies of scope and scale do matter for a least some sectors of industry. The accounting literature does not contain many studies. Banker *et al.* (1997) developed empirically a cost function for the

---

[4] See, for example, Kim (1987) who looks at multi-product economies of scale in the water supply industry. He finds that generally the industry experiences constant returns but sectors of the industry experience either economies of scale or diseconomies of scale. Tor (1996) considers the economies of scope generated by research and development in industry, finding evidence of such economies within firms. Baumol *et al.* (1988) looks at the evidence in a number of industries (pp. 494–497).

US commercial banking industry. They found that, with regard to operating costs, the factors of scale, scope and product complexity explained 38–55% of differences in operating efficiency in their sample, and that economies of scale prevailed over much of the time period involved as did economies of scope. Noreen and Soderstrom (1994, 1997) found that there were economies of scale in hospital services. BT's regulatory accounts suggest that relatively few of BT's cost pools are non-linear with volume (Bromwich and Hong, 2000, p. 144) but this may reflect a need to investigate possible cost drivers more fully.

2.3.7 Joint Costs

We discussed above the importance of joint costs in generating economies of scope within the firm. Here, we look at the problem of costing those resources that can be used jointly in the firm. Currently in accounting they are treated as fixed assets and allocated as operating or general overheads. Such allocations cannot capture their economic costs. The problems are that the costs of joint resources are often fixed costs, and that many of them will be highly specific to the firm and therefore sunk. These costs will not figure in decision making. For those joint resources which are not sunk costs, it is difficult to spread them amongst users in an economically meaningful way. Various methods have been suggested for costing these inputs. These are described in some detail in Bromwich and Bhimani (1994, pp. 107–116).

The obvious way to arrive at a cost for these inputs is to allow the users of joint resources to opt out of firm supply. The market prices available to units of the firm represent the opportunity cost of provision by the firm, and give an external validation of these activities (Faulhaber, 1975). Their use also means that any outsourcing decisions are approached on an economical basis. Such prices, where available, provide an upper bound on the internal prices that could be charged fairly to users within the firm. However they do not represent the lower bound on the firm's charges to users. This is firstly because the firm may use a superior technology to those available on the market. Secondly, in bargaining about internal charges users will argue that they should pay only the incremental cost of supplying the inputs – generally a very low cost (Sharkey, 1989, pp. 37–42). This suggests that allowing bargaining towards transfer prices for joint resources is unlikely to produce prices that are economically valid. Moreover, there is some evidence that firms are reluctant to allow major outsourcing of services provided by the firm (Drury *et al.*, 1993).

Most of the other ways of seeking to 'cost' joint resources really involve levying charges or 'taxes' on users which overall cover the costs of the extant joint resource. The ideal approach here is to ask users and potential users prior to investment how much they would pay for a share of a joint resource, that is the charge that the users said they were 'willing to bear' (Cohen and Loeb, 1982). A problem here is that it may be difficult to give potential users incentives to tell the truth, and this may require subsidies and transfers between organisational units. Another problem is that a very large amount of information from elements of the organisation is required, which may be difficult to obtain and validate. The more important problem is that the outcome of this approach reflects the result of bargaining, not the economic consequences of using a joint resource.

There is another method of charging or taxing that is less likely to run into these problems (Baumol *et al.*, 1988, Chapter 8). Here a mark-up is imposed on the variable costs of the organisational elements that use joint resources. This mark-up does not seek to levy a charge based on any notion of usage, rather it is based on what each unit is deemed 'able to bear'. This ability is defined very specifically as the ability of the quantity of the sales of organisational units to absorb price increases. The charges therefore minimise the distortion to profitability of charging for the use of joint resources. However as far as we know no firm uses this approach to costing joint costs.

A more promising approach is to recognise that joint resources do serve a number of organisational elements, and that the costs of those joint resources, if necessary for each element of production, can only be avoided if all such organisational units were closed. Thus escaping the costs of a joint resource shared by two organisational units would require both units to be shut down or to make alternative supply arrangements which also have a cost. This is shown in Figure 2.6.

Boxes A, B and C represent the variable and specific overheads of three operating units, each of which produces one product. These three operating units use a variety of joint resources, the costs of which are represented in boxes E, D and F. Joint resource E is shared by operating units B and C, that represented by D is used jointly by operating units A and B, and all three operating units utilise the corporate resource represented by F. Thus the cost of joint resource E is avoidable only if operating units B and C are shut down and escaping the cost of D requires A and B to be closed. The cost of F can only be avoided by closing the whole firm.

With this view, the total incremental cost – which equals avoidable cost in this situation – of a group of organisational units that share a joint resource includes the

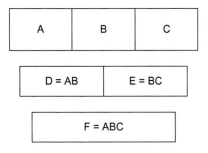

Figure 2.6   Hierarchy of Joint Costs.

variable cost of those units, their specific overheads and the cost of the shared joint resource Above, it was said that the incremental cost of a product was the total cost of the firm less the costs of the firm without the product, that is the variable costs of the product plus its specific overheads. Here, the product can be deemed worthwhile to the firm if the total revenue from the product is at least equal to its incremental cost. Joint costs are thus not part of the usual incremental cost. Where necessary joint costs exist, this test understates the incremental cost of products that share joint resources. Here, it is necessary to calculate the incremental cost of groups of products that share joint resources. Thus looking only at sharing of resource E by units B and C, this requires that the cost of the joint resource E should be included in the combined incremental cost of the product group B and C – the variable costs and specific overheads of units B and C plus the cost of the joint resource E. The product group B and C is worthwhile to the firm if the total revenue produced by their products at least covers their own incremental cost plus the incremental cost of E. The covering of cost by revenue is the only condition required to be fulfilled. No specific contribution is required from either product. This frees product managers to set prices so as to maximise their profits. Similarly, the incremental cost of the product group A and B must include the cost of unit D and yield sufficient revenue to cover this cost. The net revenues from all three units must cover the cost of unit F (Bromwich and Hong, 2000).

With this view, joint costs can adhere to any point in the organisational hierarchy. This may seem to be a little abstract but the number of resources that give rise to economies of scope is increasing in the modern economy, including many items of intellectual capital. Accountants therefore must intensify their understanding of these costs. Regulators of public utilities already have to deal with joint costs in determining reasonable prices for access by competitors to utility networks. How joint costs are assigned to services can substantially affect the prices charged to competitors (Bromwich and Hong, 2000; BT, 2006).

2.4   Strategic Management Accounting

It is not intended to review the techniques of SMA in full. A number of text books exist here (Hoque, 2006; Ward, 1997). SMA refers to a variable portfolio of mainly financial information geared towards aiding strategic decision making, although some commentators have urged that accountants should be part of the team actually formulating strategy (Bromwich, 1990). Those who urge the greater adoption of SMA have suggested rather that accountants should attempt to seek to provide more information specifically aimed at improving strategy formulation (Simmonds, 1981; Shank, 2006). In our experience, this is the view of many finance directors of large companies. The arguments for using SMA include that traditional accounting focuses strongly on the internal workings of the firm whereas it is in the market that both consumers and competitors reside. Thus both the firm as a whole and its accounting function need to look outwards to the market, for example by abandoning cost-plus pricing in favour of economic pricing. It is argued that, without SMA, costs tend to be neglected in strategic decisions where otherwise marketing and planning may dominate. Often accounting is excluded from strategic decisions, at least until the investment appraisal stage is reached, but even here it is often believed strategic factors dominate financial figures (Bhimani and Keshvarz, 1999). SMA allows a focus not only on the firm's cost structure but also on competitors' cost structures. Because of the importance of accounting information systems in Western organisations, it is argued that it is important for strategy to figure in these systems. This also allows strategy to be passed down through the organisation.

SMA information usually comprises two types (Langfield-Smith, 2008). The first provides information and estimates concerning consumer markets, including customer characteristics, and the current and future cost structures of competitors (Bromwich, 1990). This type of information illustrates the need for accountants to work with other disciplines in providing SMA-type information. This is only likely to happen if accountants are seen by other managers as business partners. The second type of information analyses the firm's value chain, focuses on the industry's value chain and considers the firm's position in this chain leading to re-engineering the firm's value chain (Shank and Govindarajan, 1993).

The usual lists of the techniques that may be used in SMA include ABC geared to strategy, costing of the product attributes offered to consumers, target costing, value accounting, competitive positioning, pricing relative to competitors, life-cycle costing, quality costing, strategic costing relative to the costs of rivals, value chain costing and benchmarking (Guilding *et al.*, 2000). That lists of this type vary between authors raises one criticism of SMA. Another criticism is that there is no agreed definition of SMA. One often-cited definition is: 'The provision and analysis of financial {and now non-financial} information on the firm's products, markets and competitors' costs, and the monitoring of the enterprise's strategies and those of its competitors in these markets over a period of time' (Bromwich, 1990, p. 28, phrase in brackets added). In our view, this disagreement concerning definitions is not of major importance; much more important is that SMA is employed by firms.

The SMA 'brand name' is not well recognised across the globe but many of its techniques are used in practice. However these may be practised either entirely by non-accountants, for example target pricing in Japan, or in combination with either business partner accountants or hybrid accountants, that is those located in operational locations but with a strong tie to the finance division. Our belief is that firms with strategic concerns need to experiment with and consider the use of those techniques of SMA which are appropriate to them using whichever staff are the most useful. Anderson (2006) shows that many disciplines produce research relevant to

SMA, which suggests many functions input into the strategy process. However, we believe that properly trained management accountants do have a major role to play. This is an area which may be contested by many disciplines, but business partner accountants may find themselves in a good position here.

The research literature on SMA is not very rich. Two field studies by Lord (1996) and Dixon (1998) suggested that SMA practices were used in highly focused situations but without accounting involvement. Experience does suggest that many managers feel traditional finance functions offer little to strategic planning and some finance functions, at least in the contemporary environment, feel that such planning takes them too far away from their core functions. A recent study of a large multinational German company did, however, find substantial use of SMA with strong involvement of controllers (management accountants) in its use and development (Tillmann and Goddard, 2008).

A leading survey article is Guilding *et al.* (2000; see also Guilding and McManus, 2002), which surveyed the use of SMA techniques in the largest companies in New Zealand, the UK, and the USA. The response rates were 51%, 38% and 13% respectively. The low response rate in the US might reflect that the functions of finance divisions there are more constrained towards financial accounting and that management accounting is coming to be regarded, at least by some commentators, as a general management skill rather than a separate profession. A number of US business schools are no longer teaching management accounting, or have reduced the amount of teaching in this area, assuming that the underlying skills are better picked up by studying core managerial disciplines (Langfield-Smith, 2008).

The Guilding *et al.* study asked about the usage of 12 SMA practices measured on a 7 point scale with '7' indicating use to a great extent. These 12 practices were classified into 3 groups:

1. those concerned with strategic costing and pricing made up of attribute, life cycle, quality, target, value chain and strategic costing and strategic pricing;

2. competitive accounting made up of competitive position monitoring, cost assessment and competitor performance based on published financial statements;

3. a group of two measures relative to brand values.

Only the usage of two techniques in the first group scored above the mid-point on the scale in the full sample. However rankings based on the perceived merit of these practices yielded much higher scores. All but one of the practices scored at mid-point or better in the full sample, with the specific techniques labelled strategic pricing and strategic costing scoring well over 5 and nearly 5 respectively. This suggests that firms are alive to the possible value of these techniques.

A more recent study of the largest Italian manufacturing firms had a sample of 93 organisations and considered the usage of 14 SMA techniques in their questionnaire

(Cinquini and Tenucci, 2007). The respondents were asked to rank these practices on a 5-point scale related to usage, where 1 equals 'never' and 5 equals 'always'. Here the scores were substantially higher than in the Guilding et al. (2000) study. Attribute costing, that is costing the provision of the characteristics that make products desirable to consumers, ranked the highest. Only two measures scored below the mid-point of the scale. As might be expected, relatively few organisations use all the techniques but most employed up to 10 of these practices. This does suggest that large firms at least should consider using and experimenting with those techniques that seem to be appropriate to them. One major defect of these surveys is the use of averages which do not tell us whether some firms, because of their characteristics, uses SMA techniques extensively and whether some firms with different attributes do not. Thus it might be expected that firms in industries with differentiated products are more likely to use SMA techniques extensively, whereas this is unlikely for firms that seek to be cost leaders – though even here it can be expected that they would use benchmarking and the cost analysis of competitor cost structures. Interestingly, none of the surveys asked questions about the use of investment appraisal in strategic decisions, where accountants would seem generally to play important roles.

The negative results with regard to the first set of techniques in Guilding et al. (2000) have been argued to suggest that SMA has not really fulfilled the promise its advocates have claimed. Recently there have been a number of articles that suggest SMA has not had a major impact on practice, at least when considered as a group of techniques. The late John Shank (2006), a pioneer and major advocate of ABC and strategic cost management (SCM) charts what he sees as the rise of strategic cost analysis in the US in the 1990s and its decline in the period 2000–2005. SCM seeks to cost a firm's value chain and the value chain for the industry as a whole, leading to reconfiguration of the firm's value chain. Shank (2006) suggests that in the 1990s, the atmosphere was exciting and conducive to the implementation of many new techniques. Many companies were experimenting with SCM, the professional bodies included SCM in their syllabi, in their journals and in their courses, and the consultants had large practices based on SCM. Surveying the scene in 2005, he seems sad that none of the companies that he had helped experiment in this area had attained a successful trajectory. He suggests that those SCM implementations that did take place in the 2000s were likely to have originated from 'shadow' accounting personnel who do not report to the chief financial officer. However, he still strongly preaches the message that accountants need to take on a strategic perspective to succeed. He still believes that 'SCM represents a conceptually superior framework for management accounting', but says 'the arguments have had their chance and have not carried the day. And so it goes' (Shank, 2006, p. 366).

Langfield-Smith (2008) provides an extensive review of the literature of SMA and the evidence of its use, and argues that SMA as such and SMA techniques have not been widely adopted (Langfield-Smith, 2008, p. 204). However much of the evidence to which she refers comes from studies of ABC adoption. Moreover she does say that many of the terms in the SMA lexicon have entered strongly the language of practice.

Even given these concerns about SMA, organisations seeking to adapt to the changing digital and global environment, especially when preparing for the post-recession world, will potentially derive value from experimentation with and use of these techniques. There is a danger that the investment and cost aspects of strategy may be considered secondary in the absence of accountants being involved in strategy and able to apply SMA techniques. In the boom years of the 1990s, some firms managed to perform well in the market without close and detailed attention to strategy. Possibly, enterprises will focus their efforts more closely on strategic issues as the economically depressed world regains momentum.

Chapter 3

Flexible Technologies, Fluid Organisations and Digitisation

▌ 3.1 Introduction

The 'fluid' organisation is a 21st century phenomenon. In less than a decade, the forces of globalisation, digitisation, technological advance and novel information exchange possibilities have altered the nature of organisational structuring and flows. Depending on business models, industries and markets, some companies today can be free from most physical asset investments and can manifest extreme flexibility and fluidity. They can be rapidly designed and then re-configured and again re-organised to tap into altering markets, products, customer segments and economic opportunities. Not only can fluid organisations alter their cost structures from high fixed cost leverage to variable cost intensity over very short time periods, but they can also redirect corporate strategy almost instantaneously alongside cost re-alignment. But organisational investments in flexibility long preceded the emergence of fluidity. The fluid organisation is a radical transition from the 20th century industrial enterprise. Its flexibility has been enabled by transitioning from a structure that is heavy in fixed assets and that has functional managerial demarcations into one that is eminently changeable and capable of real-time product shifts, service diversification and competitive re-orientation. At times, competition as well as co-operation can be present with other market incumbents.

From the early 1970s to the late 1980s, manufacturing and service enterprises invested extensively in a variety of flexible organisational technologies (FOTs). Logistics-based technologies, such as material requirements planning (MRP), developed into comprehensive rationalisation systems such as enterprise resource planning (ERP) systems (Mouritsen and Hansen, 2006). Just-in-time (JIT) purchasing and production approaches, refined in Japanese firms, were adopted in a variety of forms by enterprises in developed economies. Intelligent machines first found form as numerical control machines and subsequently, with the advent of computerised systems, they became more sophisticated as computer-aided design (CAD), testing and manufacturing systems. Flexible manufacturing systems (FMSs) investments made by some firms during the late 1980s and 1990s were conceptualised so as to enable investment in production capacity before actual products were produced and sold. A few firms sought to implement computer integrated manufacturing facilities, which represented the most extreme level of automation available during the early 1990s (Bhimani, 2008). This chapter discusses the advances which have reshaped organisations and made them more flexible and ultimately fluid. It draws out the significance of this transformation for management accounting.

3.2 A Trajectory of Flexibility

Extensive advances over a 30-year period have altered the face of service and manufacturing environments. Specifically a variety of significant changes have, over this time, been witnessed in the management of organisational resources:

- Products and services have become more diverse, thereby requiring enhanced facilities to co-ordinate and service the wider range of offerings to customers.

- The rate at which product and service innovations can be mounted and offered to customers has vastly increased. This has required new infrastructures to be developed for manufacturing, distribution, marketing and servicing of products.

- The life of products has diminished with more frequent replacements demanded. This required the search for both retail customers and industrial customers, and more capable and diversified resources and technological capabilities.

- Products have become more complex, requiring more intense design efforts and the provision of greater resources at the product inception stage. This, combined with shortening product life cycles, has led to a very high proportion of product costs being committed prior to utilisation in production or the actual incursion of costs. Facilities, technologies, marketing resources and sales infrastructures have had to be set up at the product design stages to confront products' shortening life cycles and the associated shorter time frames over which product sales could deliver profits.

- The internationalisation of trade has enabled many firms to reach wider markets, but profitability depends on the capacity to customise products to suit local tastes and needs. Thus differentiated products have attained a second further level of differentiation in local markets which further enhances the need for technologies and management resources to support intensifying differentiation.

These aspects of changing markets and products have very particular implications for cost management. Growing investments to enable diversified products to be made has led to overhead cost increases. Higher fixed cost investments into FOTs and into production capacity enhancement have translated into a growing overhead cost base as a proportion of total product costs. Investments into automated processes have reduced the need for direct labour inputs. In the mid-1980s, it was realised that these factors were creating a 'double whammy' for traditional accounting systems, which were founded on there being a majority of costs that were driven by direct labour activities. This meant that direct labour was appropriate for most allocation purposes, and there was a lower overhead cost base to begin with which could rely on volume-based allocation mechanisms. Costs in the contemporary environment were bound to be regarded as distorted by the application of traditional cost allocation rationales which were designed for very different purposes.

Enterprises with growing product diversity and production complexity would witness not only increased overhead costs but also cost growth that could not effectively be allocated under traditional means. The overwhelming existing emphasis on scale was at odds with the extensive level of scope which represented the new reality. In the mid-1980s, the popularisation of activity-based accounting was predicated on the realisation that product costs reported by traditional costing systems privileged volume over scope, which was deemed inappropriate (Ax and Bjornenak, 2007; Bhimani, 2009a; Major, 2007).

But the argument was also made that, as product innovation rates grew and as product life cycles became shorter, a doubly urgent need for timely information that was devoid of cost distortions emerged. Decisions had to be made concerning product lines, resource allocations, product offerings and prices and they had to be made fast – sometimes in real time – or market opportunities could be missed at great expense. Furthermore, the greater proportion of costs committed by the start of the production stage in a product's life cycle left little room for further cost containment post-production. Thus the onus was on managers to manage costs effectively from the beginning of the product conception stage. Cost management techniques such as target cost management, functional costing and quality function deployment matrices (see Bromwich and Bhimani, 2004) were deployed to deal with the need to link customer value and requirements to product features and functions and their costs, and to seek to achieve profitability of individual products over ever shortening product life cycles.

In general the growth of publicity surrounding an array of cost management techniques during the 1980s was a reaction to the changing nature of product markets and the more complex needs of managers. But in effect, organisational restructuring over the 1960–1990 time frame had not been extensive across most manufacturing organisations, because the nature of products had not extensively changed. Although more sophisticated products like PCs, cameras and portable CD players were developed, there was still relative constancy in product domains and organisational forms. In large part, existing industrial organisational structures remained prevalent until the early 1990s.

The rise of the fluid organisational form is a phenomenon tied to the advent of digitisation and network centricity. Following the emergence of the internet as a transformational technology, a number of important co-related changes took place. Many new products emerged which could not find form before the mid-1990s: digital cameras, iPods, HDTVs, mobile phones, etc. Whilst digital products existed prior to this time, the internet enabled their ready global access and forged their ubiquity anywhere broadband connections could be found. But in addition the 'internet economy' enabled new supply chain possibilities and the virtualisation of enterprise forms, whereby most organisational activities are carried out digitally. Products which relied on digitised data for their production and their workings could be produced by different organisations in terms of their development, production, marketing and servicing. As new products emerged, so did possibilities for the customer to engage with the firms selling the products. The consumer who had been a passive 'product taker' became, after 1995, an active 'product maker' in many contexts. And in some product categories, the customer went from being a 'price taker' to becoming a 'price maker' (see Chapter 4). Under such market circumstances, managerial tasks and organisational structures shifted. These changes will be considered here, but we first discuss FOTs which are regarded as having extensively influenced management accounting practices.

3.3   Flexible Organisational Technologies

The adoption of altered production technologies, changed work organisation approaches and digitised operating platforms result from managerial decisions to invest in change. Such decisions themselves are reflective of philosophies about what comprises desirable enterprise aims and often depend on financial evaluations of the impact of these decisions. The consequences will usually entail altered financial status in terms of the internal cost impacts of product diversity, technological complexity and operational flexibility. Ultimately a reorientation of financial management practices for controlling operational activities and decision making often also ensues.

Many technological and process-related changes have been undertaken by firms in the recent past, leading to cost impacts within their economic architecture. One important change has been in the control of quality. Other organisational alterations include investments in JIT systems, ERP, computer aided and FMSs (CAMS and FMS) and e-business technologies. We refer to changes in organisation methods, altered work-flow initiatives and digitisation-based investments in enterprises as FOTs. Quality initiatives, JIT systems, ERP and other flexible automation approaches are briefly discussed here.

3.3.1 Quality

In competitive business environments, many organisations view high quality standards as key. Formerly, quality objectives in many enterprises were confined to product quality and restricted to the shop floor where products were made. In fact quality concerns can embrace every function within organisations, from purchasing through to marketing and finance. A concern for quality entails the following considerations:

- *Accepting that the only factor that really matters is the customer*: if the customer is not happy with the product or service received then, by definition, there is room for improvement.
- Recognising the all-pervasive nature of customer/supplier relationships. Focusing on internal customers and satisfying their needs contributes to the ultimate customer's satisfaction but places responsibilities on suppliers and agents within increasingly complex supply chains.
- Moving from inspecting for conformance to a predefined level of quality to prevention of the cause of the defect in the first place – getting it right first time.
- Instead of an operator causing defects which are only recognised further down the line after quality controllers have done their inspection, making each operator personally responsible for defect-free production in their own domain. In other words, making every employee a 'quality inspector'.
- Adopting zero defect programmes, in which an extreme drive to get things right first time is pursued. This is equally applicable to activities as diverse as raising purchase orders and generating the monthly management accounts to manufacturing defect-free components in the plant – or providing total quality satisfaction in the delivery of a service.
- Deploying quality certification programmes that are based on independent third-party audits indicating the extent to which a company has complete procedural control over all its processes. If these are operating properly, they will result in the customer receiving the goods or services on time and to specification.
- Emphasising the total cost of quality as a relevant measure of all quality-related activities.

The above are considered relevant for enterprises which seek to manage the quality of processes and organisational output.

For any quality control endeavour, some notion of what constitutes quality is desirable. The quality of a product or service may be viewed as the totality of features which determine its fitness for the use intended by the customer. It is ultimately a function and a measure of customer satisfaction. It is also a reference to conformance to requirements. These and many other views on quality exist.

Often quality has to be regarded in terms that are very specific to the organisation and its customers. Customers' needs include affordability, delivery at the right time, safety, reliability and after-sales support, and one may view quality costs as falling into one of two major classes. The first category is that of the costs incurred deliberately to maintain or improve quality – the cost of conformance. It includes the costs of both prevention and appraisal activities. The second category is that of the costs suffered as a result of insufficient quality following production – that is, the cost of non-conformance – which essentially represents failure costs. Conformance deals with what could go wrong and its costs are therefore voluntary, while non-conformance deals with what has gone wrong and are thus involuntary at the production stage. Each of these categories of quality cost can further be broken down as shown in Figure 3.1.

The conformance cost of prevention refers to the cost of any action taken to investigate, prevent or reduce defects and failures. Prevention costs can include the cost of planning, setting up and maintaining the quality system, and they are incurred to reduce failures and to keep appraisal (inspection) costs to a minimum – for instance, quality planning, design and development of quality measuring and calibration and maintenance of quality measurement and tests of equipment (Dale and Plunkett, 1999).

The conformance cost of appraisal refers to the cost of assessing the quality achieved. Appraisal costs can include the costs of inspecting and testing that are carried out during the production process and on completion of the product. They are incurred in initially ascertaining conformance of the product to quality requirements, and do not include costs of re-work or re-inspection following failure. Examples are pre-production verification, laboratory acceptance testing, materials

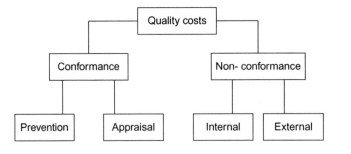

Figure 3.1 Categories of Quality Cost.

consumed during inspection and testing and the analysis and reporting of test and inspection results.

Non-conformance failure costs (internal) are the costs arising from within the organisation of the failure to achieve the quality specified. The term can include the cost of scrap, re-work and re-inspection, as well as consequential losses within the organisation. Internal costs arise from inadequate quality discovered before the transfer of ownership from supplier to purchaser. External costs arise from inadequate quality discovered after the transfer of ownership from the supplier to the purchaser. Internal failure costs may include troubleshooting or defect/failure analysis, re-inspection and re-testing, modification permits and concessions and downgrading.

Non-conformance failure costs (external) are the costs arising outside the organi-sation from the failure to achieve the quality specified. The term can include the costs of claims against warranty, replacement and consequential losses of custom and goodwill.

The possibility exists for quality management efforts to blend into existing and emerging cost management practices and thereby to integrate quality costing within internal financial control systems. A quality assurance department which is respon-sible for producing an estimate of quality-related costs might aim to involve the finance function in order to:

- prepare them for future responsibility for collecting the figures on a routine basis;
- produce figures which are valid within accepted limits of uncertainty, with the objective of establishing the major areas of quality cost – which can then be re-examined if greater accuracy is needed;
- give some measure of the cost of quality and the savings potentially achievable;
- give a means of comparison between product and product, operating unit and operating unit and possibly between the company and its competitors;
- give a baseline against which future goals can be set and improvements measured;
- propose actions to control and limit quality-related expense.

Some commonly useful sources of information for identifying and categorising quality costs are payroll analyses; manufacturing expense reports; scrap reports; re-work or rectification authorisations or reports; travel expense claims; product cost information; field repair, replacement and warranty cost reports; inspection and test records and material review records.

Organisations often perceive trade-offs between conformance and non-conformance costs. Thus if there is little or no investment in conformance costs, quality is likely to be poor and non-conformance costs will be high. Conversely, if more resources are invested in conformance activities, non-conformance costs will decrease and quality will improve. As quality improves, more difficulty will be encountered in achieving further improvement. Traditionally at the point where conformance cost is greater than non-conformance cost, any further improvement in cost reduction activity is uneconomic. There thus exists a theoretical point at which the sum of conformance and non-conformance costs is at a minimum. This conventionally has been seen as the optimal point of economic quality.

The traditional view ignores the time element of quality activities. Preventive action has no immediate impact on non-conformance. But once in place, such action can reduce non-conformance costs throughout the life cycle of the product without further investment. Repetitive appraisal and prevention have quite different effects on non-conformance costs. The traditional view of a trade-off takes no account of changes occurring over the course of time. But conformance costs can increase and only then, though with a time lag, will non-conformance costs change. So quality improvement programmes can initially seem to incur extra expenses without returns, but typically the returns from lower failure costs ultimately do emerge.

What underpins the philosophy that a lack of quality can be more costly than ensuring its presence amounts to taking a specific view on how to manage quality. The conventional view of quality management assumes that:

- Improving quality drives up time and costs.
- Defects and failures of less than, say, 10% (depending on industry) are acceptable.
- Quality should be inspected *ex-post*.
- Quality control should be a specialised and separate function.

The more recent view of quality is different in that it considers that:

- Improving quality reduces time and costs.
- The goal is zero defects and failures.
- Quality should be designed and built-in.
- Quality control should be integral to production.

The current conception of quality costs therefore suggests that there is no economic quality point other than that where the product, service or process attains 100% quality conformance. In other words, costs are minimised only when optimal quality is generated.

Although managers regularly communicate using cost-based information, they often find economic definitions about quality inconsistent with their professional mindset, or simply at odds with their cultural predisposition in thinking about organisational activities. The economics of business are often seen to be based on a knowledge and appreciation of costs. Costs may be regarded as useful in guiding the actions of financially trained managers but other managers often find operational measures, including statistical process control (SPC) and other indicators, to be good predictors and measures of quality for them. Both approaches are necessary. Quality management programmes must align with contextual preferences and the management styles of individuals if they are to achieve the desired intent. Reasons for pursuing better quality controls differ. Many companies pursue product or service quality because they believe it will improve their competitive position and, ultimately, their financial results. Others use quality as the prime competitive approach for differentiating their products or service.

Quality has many facets. One facet concerns maintaining satisfied customers who thereby remain loyal to a company which has invested in building trust through effective quality of service. The service management literature has, over the past few years, suggested that customer loyalty rather than market share drives firms' profits (Haskett *et al.*, 1997). In web-enabled firms this has significant implications. Consider, for instance, what internet shoppers go through in making a purchase. The first point of contact for a customer approaching a company website is negotiating navigation of the site. Next, the consumer attempts to retrieve desired information. Third, some customer support may be sought, perhaps in the form of a telephone call, email communication, messenger interaction or live chat. Finally, the company's logistics processes put into action the sales transaction, including packaging and shipping, payment processing, guarantee confirmation and other sales backup service. If the quality of service in the face of the price paid is deemed to be high, loyalty may be generated: if the effective navigation and information collection facilities are in place through effective development and investments in technology, this will encourage customers to purchase. The variable cost resource requirements to support customers at the pre-purchase stages usually are regarded as being low. However, if logistical problems occur once an order is placed in terms of, say, product availability, shipment or delivery or a query is raised prior to placement, this places demands on customer support mechanisms. Such demands can also cascade into more extensive logistical resource issues (returns, exchanges, cancellations) and ultimately extensive cost increases with detrimental competitive consequences.

If all aspects of logistical processes are integrated with the requisite information exchange and operational activities, a positive customer experience cycle can result. This will translate into loyalty, and this has scale effects on per unit navigation and information costs, which are largely fixed (Hallowell, 2002). The interdependencies in online purchasing and organisational processing are indicative of the extent to which internal and external failure costs are closely interrelated. Internal failures can be regarded more and more as external failures as the internet lends transparency to internal organisational processes in an attempt to be more customer-oriented. Quality costs must then adopt a different classification of what is demarcated as conformance and what is seen as non-conformance.

In contexts where customers engage in product design, the constitution of prevention costs may be subject to further alterations. In such instances, generalised conceptions of quality costing must give precedence to more realistic organisation-specific understandings of the connections between financial and cost information and quality issues. This is because it may not be possible, for instance, to speak of internal versus external quality failure costs since the production emanates from customer input.

Even modern conceptions of quality issues are constantly being reshaped. In modern manufacturing environments with complex supply chains, as well as in sophisticated service contexts and in digitised enterprise settings, the notion of quality and its related cost implications are continuously being redefined. Static management accounting approaches may survive but their original function may not dictate or drive their survival in fast-moving enterprise environments where market demands and customer requirements affect the fate of organisational information systems and their uses. It is essential then for management accountants to take contemporary notions of proper quality cost management only as a starting point, and to make modifications to suit the context on an ongoing basis.

3.3.2 JIT Systems

JIT systems for guiding operational processes have been implemented by many enterprises. JIT systems rest on the premise that production should be initiated by demand rather than prior to it. These systems in effect comprise two separate sets of activities:

1. JIT purchasing attempts to match the acquisition and receipt of material sufficiently closely with usage such that raw material stock is reduced to near-zero levels.

2. JIT production takes place only through a pull-system driven by the demand for finished products.

JIT production's aim is to obtain low-cost, high-quality and on-time production by minimising stock levels between successive processes, thereby reducing idle equipment and the deployment of facilities and workers. Some benefits of JIT purchasing include raw material stock reduction, control over delivery timing, close working relations with fewer suppliers, long-term – often informal – contracts, quality assurance and raw material/sub-component specifications. JIT production, on the other hand, stresses work-in-progress and finished goods stock reductions, decreased lead and set-up times, zero defects, a flexible workforce, continuous improvement and quality control as part of the production process and producing to order.

The underlying objective is for resources to be pulled by consumer demand rather than pushed through the organisation.

Like total quality management efforts, JIT systems emphasise the detection of production problems as they occur rather than establishing procedures for dealing with problems after production has taken place by setting aside facilities for further reconstructive processing. The 'kanban' process can support JIT production by acting as an information system through signalling devices, which relay information about changes in type and quantity of inputs at different stages of production. Kanban is a signalling system to trigger action. It historically used cards to signal the need for an item triggering the movement, production or supply of a unit in a factory. Kanban connects all aspects in the flow of manufacturing within an organisation through the provision of information about the category and quantity of materials going through the system by linking one process to the prior process. It can extend from vendors and sub-contractors to the parent firm.

Another similarity with the quality perspective on costs is that, traditionally, the stock carried by an enterprise was seen as exhibiting a trade-off between stock carrying costs and the costs of ordering. An organisation may have expectations of production levels in line with its budgeted sales. This would indicate the number of sub-components it will need suppliers to deliver. The organisation can minimise its ordering costs by ordering large quantities of sub-components infrequently and, stock them in large quantities. Alternatively, it may choose to reduce the costs of carrying large quantities of stock by ordering much more frequently and thereby absorbing the consequently higher ordering costs. One might surmise that this trade-off will indicate an optimal level of quantity to be ordered recurringly with defined frequency which will be lower in total cost terms than any other order level. Such a lower cost tallies with the notion of an 'economic order quantity'. Where the total costs incurred are the lowest, the organisation is assumed to have achieved the optimal economic order quantity. This represents the notional optimal quantity of stock to order whereby ordering and carrying costs are the lowest in total.

But under the JIT approach, this presumed trade-off does not hold. This is firstly because ordering costs can be minimised via long-term contracts with suppliers. Secondly, the carrying costs are viewed as much higher than traditionally estimated because, aside from warehousing costs and the burden of working capital tied up in the stock which are included in trade-off calculations, there are other costs to be taken into account: the stock itself may be subject to rapid obsolescence, customer tastes may change or competitors may develop substitute products.

JIT can generate new accounting approaches. One is 'backflush' accounting which not only reduces the number of conventional accounting entries in a system but, like the JIT pull philosophy, records costs backwards in allocating the cost of goods sold and stock, and does not separate out work-in-progress costs as a distinct category (see Bhimani *et al.*, 2008). The goal of 'zero-stock' manufacturing eliminates warehouse storage requirements and diminishes the need for quality and quantity inspection procedures, as well as reducing the amount of working capital tied up in stock. Such changes mean cost pools may alter considerably and allocation bases, if used at all, have to be redefined. Furthermore, under JIT purchasing factors such as quality of raw materials, availability of sub-components and reliability of supplies often take precedence over short-term price advantages. Price reductions of raw material and bought-in parts are often achieved by deploying long-term agreements with suppliers. Consequently data on purchase price variances, which may have constituted an important part of accounting-based performance measures, lose relevance in a JIT environment. Of greater relevance is not to judge the performance of the purchasing manager as an isolated activity, but to evaluate the production process as an integrated and complex set of long-term interrelated functions. This is particularly so in 'click and mortar' type organisational environments where digital purchases and other web-based triggers to internal processes, such as customer queries, have to be matched with the enterprise's infrastructure. Ultimately, JIT organisational adjustments must frequently be made 'just-in-time' to match swiftly changing market conditions.

JIT production can entail a far-reaching form of decentralisation whereby each individual worker, for instance, can halt the production process when a problem arises. This makes it doubtful that some conventional monitors like labour efficiency variance calculations have much significance in such a system. Performance evaluation indicators other than variances are also affected by the application of JIT principles. Traditionally, financial and cost management systems might report an array of monitors, such as price and efficiency variances or stock-turn ratios, on a periodic basis. But many of these are of little use given the growing importance of real-time information in enterprises today. Consequently many firms now report measures that are managerially focused on the achievement of quality objectives, reduction of stock, co-operation with vendors, on-time deliveries and process cost reduction. Measures including elapsed time, distance moved, space occupied and number of parts can be used alongside metrics concerned with quality, cycle time and product complexity. What is clear is that JIT systems alter the control and process structure of firms. Accounting may need to follow suit to provide a basis for resource monitoring and allocation as well as other managerial decisions.

3.3.3 Enterprise Resource Planning

JIT systems and quality management approaches are, to a large degree, work philosophies rather than logistical mechanisms to guide organisational processes. ERP systems allow the integration and servicing of all the different functions of an organisation by interlinking information bases. Their focus is on logistics. The precursor to

ERP for many enterprises was MRP, which sought to maximise efficiency in the timing of raw material orders and in the scheduling of machining and assembly in the manufacturing of final product. MRP systems did not, however, alter the production 'push' logic of the enterprise.

Early MRP systems depended on information based on periodic predictions, whereas later manufacturing resources planning (MRP II) systems, which integrated medium- to long-term production plans with existing and planned capacities, needed almost real-time updating. The objectives of MRP II systems included minimising all stock levels, production run disruptions, storage costs and the extra expenses incurred in accepting 'rush' orders. MRP II systems also provided forecasts of the production status of specific products and thus enabled the preparation of pro-forma statements for all categories of stock by aggregating individual product forecasts. MRP II systems made evident the need to rate vendors on price, quality and delivery.

Today an ERP system can take a customer order and provide a software 'roadmap' which automates all the relevant processes. A customer order can be linked to the customer's credit rating and order history, and to warehouse stock levels and transportation logistics via the ERP. Such order road-map 'views' may be made accessible to any department that needs the information. ERP's aim is to provide instant access to all data generated by widely scattered and functionally diverse organisational units and sites. The compatibility of ERP systems with digitised business processes has expanded over the past few years. Where, traditionally, software solutions specialised in accounting ledgers and related information processing, they now extend to human resources, marketing, manufacturing and distribution modules. At the core of ERP software there is a central database, which may physically be dispersed rather than centralised, that feeds data into modular applications operating on a standard computing platform.

Rather than just seeking to customise the product to the customer the enterprise can, via an ERP, determine how far to customise the whole service to that individual customer based on analyses of perceived future gains. An ERP system can seek to make this possible through customer relationship management (CRM) system linkages.

Naturally the perceived needs following on from an ERP system's objectives may be highly organisation-specific. But, in general, the following are common reasons for companies to implement ERP:

- Integrate financial information
- Standardise and speed-up manufacturing processes
- Reduce stock through better co-ordination and allocation of resources
- Standardise human resources information
- Integrate customer order information.

In the early 1990s, organisations entered the era of the networked enterprise. Different information needs for different departments and functions had to be met by a single unified software approach with diverse modules to interface the information generated by traditional stand-alone systems. Consider, for instance, Valentino Fashion Group which acquired a series of brands over two decades including Marlboro Classics, Missoni, Lebole and Hugo Boss among others. Their information interface problem became evident in 2005: its business units were running separate IT systems and databases. Valentino regarded it as a strategic imperative for the company to create a single IT infrastructure centralising human resources, administrative, financial and operational processes. A key objective was fast access to information to control the supply chain. As noted by group Chief Information Officer, Patrizio Buda:

> *High fashion is extremely complex. There are thousands of mandates in each of our processes, and we handle high-value items that go through many stages. So things do get lost. What we need is a way to allow creative people the time they need, but then get goods into stores as quickly as possible. (Information Age, May 2008, p. 31)*

With complete deployment of the ERP in Europe and the US, Valentino could track orders, merchandise and business processes across the organisation, with improved forecasting and management reporting. The ERP system gave management insight into where efficiencies could be possible. Luca Vianello, General Manager of Valentino Fashion Group, pointed out that:

> *We can easily get new sites on-line, or close warehouse facilities very quickly if they aren't efficient. (Information Age, May 2008, p. 31)*

For most firms, the integration of information systems focuses on a multitude of business processes and cuts across many established functions (Granlund and Malmi, 2002). This necessitates an understanding of not just organisational processes and functions, but also the organisation's capacity to undergo change. Determining the level of investment the enterprise makes in developing the requisite information design, expertise and knowledge concerning systems integration issues is a key challenge for management accountants. It can be difficult to quantify precisely the costs and particularly the benefits of readier access to information or different information views. But generally expected benefits have been dealt with as qualitative and strategic returns in management accounting practice and in management in general.

Where information systems architecture changes, conventional notions of effective control become outmoded. Problems arise where systems retain the basis of control priorities from the past. Thus where ERP attempts to create 'end-to-end' systems for an entire organisation, control approaches need to be revised.

Change is part of the environment in which enterprises operate and, with the advent of internet-based technologies, they will increasingly be faced with opportunities that require use of the internet to link with their suppliers, trading partners and customers. Such changes are forcing a shift of emphasis from the internal focus that is typical of ERP systems to an increasingly externally oriented one. This enhances the importance of both business-to-business and front-office applications. Solutions which are more comprehensive than the structured logic of ERP systems may be required in the future. The outward focus which is increasingly evident in business environments across the globe, and which is buttressed by digital technologies, underscores the potential relevance of thinking strategically about information systems investments.

3.3.4 Flexible Automation

Whilst technology costs are generally decreasing and the range of functions achievable by any one system is increasing, it is becoming more important for software structures to be re-configurable and to enable flexibility and adaptability (Dechow *et al.*, 2007). From the early 1990s, many organisations invested in FMSs. These consist of programmable machines and devices that work together within an entire factory or in certain areas of an organisation. Their component elements can comprise robots, measuring and material-handling equipment and machine tools that all operate automatically under the control of computers. FMS rely on computer-automated systems to transport parts, tools or other products across different points on factory floors and assembly lines. Harmon (2009) notes that, to operate flexible manufacturing technology, computer programming language must be used to allow the machines and devices to communicate with each other firstly as to when and where to transfer different materials and secondly as to the schedules for starting and stopping flexible manufacturing programs. FMS can also allow the making of new parts that were not conceived at the time of investing in the system. The combination of high capital outlay costs to implement FMSs and the expertise to run them affect the cost structures of firms which invest in them.

The use of FMSs in many automated environments assumes a high degree of integration with other manufacturing and organisational activities. An ERP system will naturally take account of changes in the deployment of an FMS. For many years, customers, both industrial and retail-based, have used CAD technologies to customise products within preset parameters. Such computer generated designs (and sometimes computer aided tests) are sometimes linked to computer assisted manufacturing (CAM). The concurrent use of automated handling systems for subcomponents, stock retrieval and other complex FMS allowing a high diversity of production possibilities will impact organisational cost functions and have cost management implications. Increased overhead costs will ensue with FMS investments, and production diversity may increase the number of cost pools and extent of both volume-based cost drivers and non-volume ones. This could trigger a need for more costing sophistication.

The main advantages of an FMS over a traditional factory organisation structure include the ability to produce differing varieties and volume levels of products, quicker customer response and reduced labour costs as materials-handling systems and automated storage and retrieval systems replace labour. In addition there are savings from the automation of manufacturing processes, which also cut down on human operators. Where industrial robots are used there is a clear reduction in labour costs and the minimisation of errors, with workers freed from having to perform dangerous or merely repetitive tasks.

The decision to use FMSs such as robots or CAD/CAM technology is difficult to analyse using conventional financial capital appraisal techniques because of the wide array of intangible benefits that are implicated which are not easy to quantify. These may include improved design drafts, better customer perception of products, increased productivity and morale of employees and enhanced product quality. Cost control in FMS settings is also problematic because of the difficulty of setting labour standards for certain salaried expertise-intensive activities. Moreover, with learning, over time, these activities result in increased productivity and reduced operational time requirements, which generate the need to continuously update standards. Product costing is simplified when engineering and design costs can be ascribed to the production of a specific order. Performance measures can be tied to improving set-up times, materials usage and manufacturing time, defect rates, product versatility and quality – for which no simple measures exist, but in respect of which there is a need for customisation for different production contexts (Hansen and Mouritsen, 2007).

The use of robots during the 1990s was problematic to the extent that a minor adaptation in production required taking a robot cell or group of robots carrying out specific tasks offline, which was very disruptive. But today offline software applications permit engineers to program robots and to make adjustments remotely without disrupting production. This means that designing and bringing a new product to the market takes less time. Whereas it could traditionally take car manufacturers 4–7 years to bring a car to market from design to production, with advances in software applications companies such as Toyota are aiming to cut the product development cycle to just 1 year. The advent of FMSs in which technology gains in robotics hardware and software applications are integrated has led firms to leverage this as a core competitive advantage. The ability remotely and dynamically to orchestrate many aspects of design and production using computers, including gathering real-time data on manufacturing processes and distributing it over the internet to various links in the supply chains, provides some enterprises with a strategic edge. Broadly product quality, set-up times, machine utilisation, stock levels, space and production information are all affected by automated production technologies which enhance flexibility.

Some manufacturing organisations have attempted to invest in plants that utilise totally computer integrated manufacturing operations using negligible levels of labour resource. Such facilities offer a level of technological flexibility that is essential in product markets characterised by extremely short product life cycles. They provide the necessary capability to alter and perhaps extend product life cycles, which may be a core strategy for organisational survival. In such environments, market opportunities that permit the attainment of desired levels of profitability may be of short duration. Developing appropriate strategic financial management expertise to recognise such market opportunities quickly, and to mobilise manufacturing design and production correspondingly, is becoming part of organisations' essential core strengths. Production technologies that permit flexibility across corporate internet-based systems place enhanced pressure on organisations to understand and manage costs across business-to-business boundaries. Such changes are influencing the design of financial management systems in organisations across many industries.

3.4 Organisational Structure as Strategy

As noted above, operational techniques and technologies have altered the production of goods and the provision of services. Enterprises continuously innovate products, and change production techniques and how they compete in increasingly intense markets that are subject to globalising forces and effects. Where competitive strength becomes less sustainable through product characteristics, some firms opt to differentiate their design and structure more than their products. Firms within the same industry opt for different architectures in terms of their organisational configurations. Thus Dell employs a design strategy which markedly differs from HP. Likewise SAP has structured itself in a manner very distinct from Oracle. Tesco manages its suppliers in ways that are very different to Wal-Mart's supply management logistics. Zara, the clothing retailer, takes a different view on vertical integration compared to Gap. How these firms adopt highly differentiated internal structuring approaches in relation to their competitors is key to organisational survival.

The advent of digital technologies and globalisation enhances the potential of enterprises to achieve differentiation of enterprise structure, even though products may be very similar. Though it has been argued that organisational re-design can be resource-intensive, its rewards in terms of profits, costs and lower risks often surpass investments in product design and other strategic initiatives (Bryan and Joyce,

2007). Building strategy via organisational design is an evolutionary step away from the organisational strategies of the 20th century when capital, labour and land were the scarce resources, and vertical hierarchical structures and extensive expertise-focused management hierarchies were regarded as fundamental to efficient performance. Bryan and Joyce (2007, p. 78) note that:

> *Today's companies must redesign themselves to remove unproductive complexity while simultaneously stimulating the effective and efficient creation and exchange of valuable intangibles. They must be able to mobilise mind power as well as labour and capital.*

Changing the organisation so as to mobilise the intellectual capital of the workforce and tap into their knowledge, relationships and skills capacities requires firms to seek ways to create sources of new wealth at relatively lower levels of risk (Roberts, 2006). Altering organisational designs can trump the gains generated by other, more traditional strategic initiatives. But such organisational design changes must also be supported by alterations in information systems, including accounting information flows, to adapt to the changing managerial needs and control requisites that the organisational re-design implicates (Merchant and Van der Stede, 2007). As organisations become more 'knowledge management'-orientated, the focus may turn to maximising returns on people instead of just on capital. This translates into creating organisations that continuously adapt and evolve. If traditional structures give way to fluid enterprise designs, then the management accountant may react by re-designing control approaches.

3.5 Risk Management as Strategy

Increasingly, risk management as a formal practice is becoming a priority for firms. Risk is now seen as an almost ubiquitous concern for enterprises. The emergence of risk concerns and risk categories has a multitude of roots and reflects multiple interests (Power, 2007). Risk and strategy are interlinked in many firms in a formal manner. This is certainly so at board level, where use may be made of the strategic scorecard (see Chapter 4). A clearly defined strategy is considered essential by some commentators for an appropriate risk management function. The presence of appropriate risk management sets the boundaries within which strategy can be pursued.

Nagumo and Donlon (2006), for instance, illustrate a strategy for increasing revenue and a strategy for productivity. The risk for an 'increase revenue' strategy may consist of entering new business territories through corporate acquisition, direct foreign investment to penetrate new markets, targeting a new customer segment and launching new products. In addition to external marketing activities, the strategy will have to be promoted internally and involve personnel becoming more results-oriented. When considering the implications of implementing this strategy, the authors suggest that the following risks may require assessment:

- Business failure due to management's lack of know-how about the new business area.
- Sudden increase in country risk due to deterioration of conditions in the target country.
- Failure of new product development due to unanticipated changes in customer preferences.
- Morale issues due to hastily implemented results-oriented policies.
- Increased profit volatility as a result of specific risks.

Some authors regard it as possible to think about the relationship between strategy and risk management by integrating them into the BSC (Kaplan and Norton, 2008), and by examining the Committee of the Sponsoring Organisation for the Treadway Commission (COSO) Enterprise Risk Management (ERM) framework. In September 2004, COSO announced a new ERM as an enhancement to the previous version, the COSO Internal Control Framework of 1992. The COSO ERM is a three-dimensional model consisting of four management objectives, eight components of risk management and the organisational units involved in these. The model systematically analyses the risk that accompanies implementation of a strategy, and seeks to manage the risk to a tolerable level.

When the COSO ERM objectives are examined, it can be seen that they are similar to the areas covered by the internal process perspective of the BSC.

- 'Strategy' objectives correspond to what is covered in the BSC's strategic themes, such as product leadership, complete customer solutions, low cost operations, etc.
- 'Operations' objectives refer to 'strategy' cascaded down to the operational level.
- 'Reporting' objectives correspond to financial reporting; corporate social responsibility (CSR) reporting; communication with shareholders, authorities and external stakeholders and building a brand image.
- 'Compliance' objectives correspond to the basic requirements in terms of regulatory compliance for good corporate citizenship.

The eight COSO ERM components can also be mapped out, according to Nagumo and Donlon (2006). For instance the 'internal environment' indicates how the management team perceives the importance of risk management, and this corresponds to the BSC's goal to mobilise change through executive leadership – this is one of the principles of the strategy-focused organisation. And 'objective setting', according to these commentators, corresponds to clarifying strategy, which is a primary BSC function addressed through the strategy mapping activity.

There are numerous issues that require careful thinking if an enterprise is to implement the BSC linked with ERM. Indeed a variety of concerns associated with the BSC and linkages with other enterprise activity dimensions have been voiced (Norreklit and Mitchell, 2007). In many organisations, the BSC and risk management are both in the process of becoming formal mechanisms to deal with strategy and risk management. The potential for integrating the two will become an issue where risk is not conceptualised in terms that are compatible with strategy, and *vice versa*. A similar integration has been attempted in prescriptive calls for linking management accounting and strategy (see Chapter 2). The assumption has been made that management accountants can in fact improve strategic thinking, planning and processes. The viability of such a perspective is linked to many assumptions that see technical and operational issues as not being influenced by organisation-specific factors. But many factors that are cultural, political, professional, educational and institutional impact on the ability to achieve operational intentions. In noting that 'management accounting and finance professionals should seize the opportunity to become partners with senior management and the board in ERM implementation', the US's Institute of Management Accountants acknowledges that 'an effective process tailored to each organization's unique culture' is also essential (IMA, 2007, p. 27). The presumption of a desirable role in the associations between management accounting and strategy, or for hybridising expertise and for a directional and prescriptive role for management accountants, is not unproblematic. Much research is indicative of this (Ahrens and Chapman, 2005; Bhimani and Langfield-Smith, 2007; Chua, 2007; Kurunmaki and Miller, 2006; Miller and O'Leary, 2005; Roslender and Hart, 2003; Vaivio, 1999). In a similar manner, the complex links between concerns with managing risk and management accounting are only now beginning to find articulation in management accounting writings and practice (Bhimani, 2009b). The nature of the relationship between risk management and management accounting will take time to gain clarity.

3.6   Rethinking the Boundaries of Management Accounting

As management accounting has become more connected to managerial processes, including strategy and risk management, the role of the management accountant is viewed within the profession across the different countries where it exists as a distinct occupational expertise: less as a support and more as a 'hands-on' line management activity. In many organisations, the IT function is likewise no longer viewed purely as a staff function providing technological support, but as a line activity providing business solutions and decisions. Consider the following illustrations of changes being put into place in some large enterprises.

The consolidation of back-office functions such as Finance and Human Resources into Global Business Services (GBS) at Procter and Gamble (P&G) brought about huge cost savings, and created a novel way of making such functions more profit-centred and decision-responsible rather than simply serving an information provision role to decision makers. The important difference is that GBS involves IT being regarded not as a provider of technology but as a provider of possible business decisions and solutions. Consider CAD and CAT systems, which were widely invested in by firms wishing to use IT in producing and testing product prototypes. The objective was to innovate faster and more cheaply than the traditional method of physically producing and testing real product prototypes. P&G's Information and Decisions Solutions unit within GBS extended this idea through modelling and simulation. Instead of creating consumer products as physical mock-ups which are placed on supermarket shelves to attempt to engage consumer focus groups and retailers in new product developments, virtual reality technology use enables multiple new benefits including cost savings, time-to-market speed-up and customer input into both product creation and purchasing experience. Filippo Passerini, the President of GBS and Chief Technology Officer of P&G, explains that:

One technology centers on a room with all walls covered by high resolution screens that create a full, three-dimensional world. By using a pointer you sense that you're moving through the aisles of a real store even though you are standing still. The renderings of products on shelves look more real than the real thing. Engagement with the customer is much more immediate and profound. More importantly, this technology allows us to quickly implement feedback on a product's packaging and artwork. Instead of taking five to six weeks to redesign a physical mock-up, we do it in days. This allows us to iterate more times and still cut costs while bringing innovation to market much faster and better (quoted in Bloch and Lempres, 2008, p. 15).

Consider too the example of Dell. In 2006, Dell was losing market share to rivals like HP and its profits were down 28% from the previous year. Negative sentiment, according to a Dell-commissioned survey, was 48%. The main problem was that: 'On tech blogs and consumer forums, Dell had become almost a by-word for lousy customer service ... the company simply became arrogant and set in its ways' (Fortt, 2008, p. 19). The company set up a learning team engaging with customers on Twitter, Facebook and other social media sites, and invited customer input via the Dell site 'IdeaStorm'. Here individuals could offer suggestions and vote for the ideas of others. This 'wisdom of the crowd' approach led to Dell's Latitude laptop line, with its customer-suggested light-up keyboard, faster connection, longer battery life and wide colour choice. Within 2 years, the company's profit margin rose from 16.6% to 19.1% and its negative customer sentiment had decreased to 23%.

The use of advancing internet technologies, combined with changing attitudes to the internet, have altered the traditional boundaries of organisations towards becoming more fluid by enabling customer input into what might in the past have been limited to the tight confines of the research and development department and focused market research. While the internet initially provided access to virtually unlimited information, the transition is increasingly not simply the provision of information but the enablement of knowledge production and access. As Ford (2008, p. 45) notes: 'The most important thing to understand about Web 2.0 is that it refers to the web as a platform rather than a depository'. Ultimately, internet users can deploy it to allow them to create content. Content creation becomes the engine of organisational knowledge for enhanced performance in many contexts (this is discussed further in Chapter 4).

Cost management approaches have, in the past two decades, increased the links between producers and consumers in terms of making product specifications align better with customer requirements. To a degree this has affected the extent to which organisations share practices across borders, become more homogeneous and show signs of convergence (Busco *et al.*, 2007). Target cost management and functional analysis techniques have sought to enable enterprises to align the cost of resources to generate specific product dimensions with the perceived value of those dimensions to the customers. This has led to product re-design on the basis of the identification of variances between, on the one hand, resource consumption providing product benefits and, on the other, the value of these benefits as perceived by customers. In terms of pricing, organisational production processes have been re-designed and re-shaped, taking the price as the starting point, allowing for a required profit and structuring production to meet cost limits. Quality functional matrices have also enabled enterprises to prioritise product improvements based on customer perceptions of priority product dimensions. These and other management accounting practices have brought enhanced alignment between enterprise activities and market needs, by creating explicit channels and structures for mediating information flows across organisational boundaries between producers, suppliers and customers.

In broad terms, the past decade has exposed organisations to a wide variety of changes ranging from increasing flexibility and fluidity to the growing impact of digitisation. Enterprises themselves have been the drivers of these changes, impacting the activities of firms with which they interface directly as well as indirectly with other firms. A consequence of this for management accountants in practice and for management accounting professional bodies and commentators has been to lend support to and to instigate and promote a variety of changes.

The ongoing transformation of the management accounting field is inevitable and in many regards desirable. The consequences are many. Research and investigations will reveal the extent of the nature and impact of this transformation. It is likely that there will be new approaches and techniques which will surface. These will come from practitioners, educators, researchers and consultants. Prescriptions will be experimented with in practice and novel outcomes will emerge (Ahrens and Chapman, 2007; Chua, 2007; Cooper *et al.*, 1981; Otley, 2006; Scapens, 2006). Judgments and analysis of the degree to which novel management accounting 'solutions' are worthwhile will be documented, which will prove to be of potential value to some practitioners.

But beyond this, the field of management accounting is likely to see more changes. In an increasingly globalising, integrated and technologically connected world, organisations will witness an accentuated and accelerated exchange of information, expertise and knowledge. The lessons will emerge faster and very possibly in a manner that is less cognisant of traditional functional demarcations between what comprises management accounting and what does not. Inevitably this will lead to alterations in what management accounting is deemed to entail. These changes are likely to be both affected by enterprise-specific factors and to be institutionally influenced.

A significant consequence will be the education of future management accountants. The technical precepts studied in management accountancy programmes will alter. But in addition, the ability of management accountants to understand other areas and to integrate them with the work, tasks and objectives of the changing management accounting function will be key.

Flexibility, fluidity and the advent of digital technologies are core features of the changing nexus of organisational activities. Management accounting as a field will seek to explore the significance of such changes for its future growth.

Chapter 4

Cost Co-creation and Globalisation

█ 4.1 Introduction

The previous chapters were concerned with the path of change that the field of management accounting followed in the past, and sought to explain ongoing changes and to project into the future how the thrust of transforming forces will play out. This chapter considers a variety of other phenomena affecting management accounting. It offers an analysis of specific emerging forces shaping the field as they surface from observations of practice and as discussed by some management commentators. The chapter brings together various observations and commentaries to depict the nature of influences which are affecting the field in ways which have not been extensively identified or discussed by writers in management accounting. One key element of change relates to the way in which information is produced as an input to decision making. This concerns the growing 'fuzziness' in information production and the divide that was traditionally presumed to exist.

█ 4.2 The Finance Function and Information 'Pull'

The increasingly osmotic boundaries of organisations which enable the permeation of outside market forces into the organisation's field of activities, and the transfer of information and products to the market from the organisation, can be seen as reflective of the philosophy of JIT systems. The premise of JIT is to re-orient production and purchasing activities to match the buying behaviour of a firm's customers, rather than adopt the 'push-based' approach of businesses producing in the expectation that inventory not yet demanded by a customer will ultimately meet with a sale. The 'pull' philosophy of JIT (discussed in Chapter 3) represents the triggering of organisational resource flows by forces that are external rather than internal to the enterprise. This is deemed to make corporate resource utilisation more efficient and to enable the achievement of enhanced financial performance whilst better meeting customer and market needs. Both traditional management and JIT systems presume organisational boundaries that make precise distinctions between the enterprise, its suppliers and its customers. But in addition JIT encourages a collaborative, rather than a traditional and individualistic, model of value chain harmony between enterprises, which leads to legal contracts based on the comprehensive description of items to be purchased and supplied. JIT systems are considered to work best when aligned with compatible accounting structures, such as the 'backflush' accounting philosophy which reflects a 'pull' rather than a 'push' representation of economic transactions and flows. But the JIT philosophy is also echoed within the finance function in more fundamental ways.

Visualising an enterprise's information flows as following a 'pull' rather than a 'push' philosophy is increasingly evident in many companies. Information systems allow managers, on an individual basis, to determine and customise the information they require for operational control purposes, for *ad hoc* decision making and for strategic management. Rather than seeing the finance function as a purveyor of pre-determined and pre-defined accounting reports conveyed indiscriminately to managers, customised and user-designed financial control information is regarded as an essential and growing product of not just finance departments but also other integrated business information functions. In other words, the finance function is, in many organisations, adopting a JIT-like 'pull' rather than 'push' philosophy in its provision of information.

Consider, for instance, P&G's Global Business Services (GBS) division which was briefly discussed in Chapter 3. GBS operates an integrated service whereby 'operating units can come to us and say: "A retailer is coming in, and these are the products we want to show". We take care of the whole process end-to-end by building the virtual store and running the actual session'. (Filippo Passerini, in Bloch and Lempres, 2008, p. 15). GBS represents a function which delivers information needs to internal consumers of information on a customised 'pull' basis. Information users are, like customers in a JIT environment, capable of pulling resources – in the form of information – through the organisation. Of relevance is the ability of individual users not simply to trigger information movements but to customise the formatting and structuring of information to suit their needs and desires. Information users within organisations increasingly partake in the information-making exercise. Managers are becoming information-makers or information-producers through advanced decision support information systems.

The implications for management accounting are significant. An ongoing aim of professional management accountancy bodies since at least the late 1990s has been to promote for the profession a line role rather than purely a staff support role. The management accountant, it is thought, should be mobilising action following formal and direct input into decision making. Monitoring the outcome of organisational action and engaging in control and reporting activities should also engage the management accounting function. In the context of managers becoming information-producers across an array of enterprise activities, the management accountant has, to a degree, an unintended head-start. Technology and flexible enterprise resources, including novel digitised information networks, have altered the potential of the management accountant's input into organisations. The management accountant's growing input into decision making in many contexts corresponds to the broader notion of managers increasingly becoming information-producers with the help of information specialists. This then is a trend which will drive the field further and facilitate its aim to create, provide, use and act on financial, strategic, operational and control-associated enterprise information.

4.3   Customers as Product-Makers and Co-creation

The notion of managers increasingly customising information as a decisional resource to suit their needs is an adaptation to information user needs which could be anticipated, given the complex production and market environments which have altered the way enterprises now function. Advances in information technologies, combined with the plummeting costs of information production and retrieval and the falling costs of hardware, are facilitating user design input into information production. The need for real-time user-focused information, and the concurrent availability of technology, has accelerated the transition of process information functions within firms. What has been less predictable is the growing input of customers in the design of products. Many companies today cannot envisage product design without the customers' input in a very fundamental way to the core of the product's design (Bettencourt and Ulwick, 2008; Gulati, 2007).

Historically, markets moved from being producer-focused to somewhat consumer-driven during the 1960s and 1970s across many large firms with the consumer who initially accepted both price and product forms becoming, to a degree, a price-maker (Hippel, 2005). The entry of low-price Japanese products in particular into Western markets offered consumers choices and forced many firms to price more competitively to retain or grow their markets further. Producers focused on product-making and customers became price-makers in some industries.

However the products being purchased from the Far East competed not just on price but also on quality. Higher-quality products, offered initially at high prices, became more competitively priced by Western producers in the late 1970s. This stemmed especially from a realisation that enhancing quality in production environments did not necessarily increase costs: high quality did not necessitate a cost trade-off. Thus customers sought higher quality at existing prices and so firms reacted by competing on a higher-quality/lower-price footing (Dale and Plunkett, 1999).

Some level of parity was reached with high-quality, low-priced products being offered by many competing firms across many markets.

Ultimately, high quality/low price became a starting point for economic viability in some industries. During the 1980s, many firms then sought to increase their competitiveness by enhancing the level of customer service provided. In the 1990s, firms found it important to offer value while offering high-quality products and high customer service, but continued to face competition based on competitors providing more product characteristics and a more differentiated, sophisticated and demanding customer base. This required localised customisation of otherwise standard products across the globe. Engaging the customer in defining the product was key to competitive appeal, but opportunities for doing so were limited.

The rise of the internet from the mid-1990s provided novel opportunities for firms to increase their interface with customers. Although the customer over the prior three decades evolved from being a price-taker to a price-maker and, to a degree, ultimately influenced quality, product diversity and customer service, it was not until the advent of e-business technologies that companies could develop a way of competing by turning customers into product-makers. Today a large number of organisations no longer regard customers as product-takers. For instance, many social internet sites rely entirely on user-generated content.

Firms can operate websites where customer experiences increase interfacing and consumer engagement, and enhance the customer's ability to define the product and, indeed, to extend what counts as the product. For instance, an auction site such as eBay offers a basic service to make purchases but also enables a 'thrill of the kill' purchasing experience for the winning bidder. Staging customer experiences has become an avenue for allowing customer input to be coupled with providing entertainment. Amazon.com allows users to inform other users about their views of products and also to cast judgment on Amazon and its affiliate suppliers. The consumer evaluation of products widens Amazon's appeal as a seller with a unique platform which is difficult for competitors to match. Customers on some travel airline sites can express their wishes concerning a flight and offer a price for the product which the airline can decide to accept or to decline. Other sites allow consumers to design their desktops, golf clubs, dolls, etc. online prior to purchase. In such contexts, where customers can influence both the nature of the product and its price, conventions of cost control and cost functions have to be revisited. The roles of costing are likely to change with changes in customer input into organisational activities.

There are other illustrations of internet-based platforms where customer input is especially prevalent. The internet allows digital products to be created. For instance, multi-player online dancing sites allow players to create 'avatars' (virtual persons) and dance with other such avatars. Dancing takes place via tapping fingers on appropriate keyboard keys or using a USB-attached floor mat for real dancing. Such strong engagement brings about customer 'stickiness' to the site and encourages 'word of mouth' market growth. Other platforms such as Flikster.com, Facebook. com, MySpace.com and Wikipedia.com invite users to generate content which they then 'consume'. Consumers thus co-innovate products and services with producers and become 'pro-sumers' (Tapscott, 2009, p. 11). Such companies 'must organise a constantly shifting global web of suppliers and partners to do the job' (Colvin, 2008, p. 16). The partners can include customers.

Many successful companies are now less inclined to invent entirely new products and services independently of consumers. Rather, they create the products *with* the customer and seek to generate a new experience in the process. This arises in part because no enterprise can fathom all the unique experiences sought to be created and experienced by customers.

Although enterprises may not pre-design the consumer experience with the product, they still invent the product concept and orchestrate achievement of the product's potential via the consumer. Thus, Apple Inc invented the iPod but users create their own experiences with the product by loading it with independently created content: podcasts, shows, music, etc. Facebook.com likewise developed the platform for users to stage their own unique experiences. But both involved both 'customers' and other 'suppliers' who create software applications. The user experience is effectively 'co-created' (Prahalad and Krishnan, 2008). Co-creation of products is not a choice but a necessity for many business models because the product choices are infinite and cannot be conceptualised or delivered by one 'producer'.

This movement necessitates management control premises which depart from the traditional model of organisations themselves monopolising the design processes to create products and services and manage owned resources. For the finance function, this implies the production of information relating to the provision of co-created products where innovation potential is not owned entirely by the firm. It also means that the product of the finance function itself must be subjected to co-creation with information users. This requires some rethinking of cost management systems. Costing the product and its production is subject to different sources of input and prior analyses. The product revenue potential is also not directly associated with the source of revenues where, for instance, advertisers pay for juxtaposition alongside the 'product'. Search engine results and 'ad-links' are examples.

Industrial firms like LEGO have attempted successfully to engage in 'distributed co-creation', whereby customers are invited to suggest new products and be financially rewarded if their ideas prove profitable. Likewise Peugeot sought design input from the public and built a demonstration model of the winning design, which ultimately led to the creation of a video game involving a consumer-designed vehicle. Such a model only partially engages the user in contributing to product development; digitised products can offer much more scope for greater customer participation. The online encyclopedia, Wikipedia for instance, is created entirely by its users. In such cases, control processes which traditionally are seen to be internal to the organisation must be ceded to networks of participants, including suppliers and customers; online content 'quality controls' can be mounted by designated users, for instance. Giving control to a mix of users and suppliers is now often regarded as essential within new business models sustained by novel web-based technologies.

IBM has adopted the open operating system Linux for some of its computer products and systems. Linux in this context draws upon a core code base which is continuously enhanced and improved by a wide-ranging community of systems software developers, of which only a minority work for IBM. Thus different companies will use co-creation with different mixes of inputs from different parties. But 'what facilitates this new approach to innovation is the rise of the web as a participatory platform' (Bughin *et al.*, 2008).

Broadly speaking, open innovation and co-creation (Chesbrough, 2006; Prahalad and Krishnan, 2008) will continue to necessitate the rethinking of enterprise control structures. For the management accounting field, there are two immediate effects. First, sources of revenue may possibly be separated from the product's costs. Profit drivers may be triggered by consumption but the product consumed may actually have a zero price. Customer input into the product design implies the need to reconsider pricing strategy. In contexts where what is produced is not what generates income, the notion of cost-based pricing becomes much less relevant. Market-based price setting will retain relevance where revenue generators face competition, but the link to organisational cost incursion will remain indirect. Consequently cost allocation will have different objectives where this is undertaken. The disconnect between pricing and product costs (see below) will imply altered cost objects and altered cost management objectives.

The second effect is that while cost containment will continue to be a key concern for any organisation, the consumer's input into product design will re-define cost containment rationales. For instance, a firm may wish to invest large fixed costs to provide a specific and attractive experience for customers, but it may decide to focus, as a consequence of such investments, on customers who are familiar with using web-based platforms and technology. Concurrently, the cost of customer assistance – which may have a high variable cost such as phone lines, messenger and ring-back services – may be pared down. Thus the cost structure will delimit the possible strategies pursuable by a firm. Conversely, the strategic objective of the firm will itself potentially influence the nature of the cost structure. What is clear is that strategy, cost and technology inter-linkages within modern firms today create inter-connections which have not been present in the past. Consequently management accountants will need to adapt to a broader vision of their role in complex organisational contexts. This could include partnering with managers, rather than simply providing information and being dissociated from decision making and action implementation.

4.4   The Changing Price–Cost–Product Interface

Two major forces have extensively altered the scope of business and organisational possibilities since the late 1990s: the expansion of digitisation and the accelerating pace of globalisation. In relation to internet technologies and the growth of the digital economy, it is widely acknowledged that it takes more than just technology to profit from technology (Afuah and Tucci, 2003; Hippel, 2005), and that technology is rarely on its own the key to unlocking economic value since 'companies create real wealth when they combine technology with new ways of doing business' (Manyika *et al.*, 2008, p. 61).

Pricing is directly linked to a firm's profits. Pricing issues have traditionally been an important domain of management accountants' tasks. The long-term transition away from cost-plus pricing towards competition- and market-based price determination and the associated target pricing strategies have all been reflective of changes in the competitive markets for products and services, as well as the changing nature of production, delivery and servicing. New conceptions of costs that have moved away from job order and process-based costing to activity-based costs and target-focused costs are now guiding pricing decisions. A key element of stability in the past amidst such changes in costing and pricing approaches was that the product remained definable and its characteristics were to a large degree tangible.

The demarcation of many products' boundaries in the digital economy has now become more nebulous. Digital products for instance may include both entertainment and functionality. Purchasing a product on eBay can engage the consumer in an auction process which broadens the product boundaries to encompass the buying experience. A great many products, as explained above, are co-created between enterprises and consumers. In some cases, the consumer creates the entire product on an enterprise-designed platform. Consider Facebook.com, which aims to become the 'planet's standardised communication and marketing platform' (Hempel, *Fortune* 2.3.09, p. 36). The site allows users to create a multitude of facades – sharing photos, joining clubs and interacting with others – and also gives users controls over the amount of information they are able to share with others. The new business model and its platform for letting the consumer design the product they consume on a platform they control to a degree has enabled value creation over a very short span of time. The company did not achieve break-even in its first 5 years of operation, but it attained 175 million users and its 'consumer' base was then growing at 5 million per week. As noted, users of Facebook.com create the product they consume. The company establishes a platform to enable this and adds features to make the 'product' appealing and continuously changing. The opportunity for users to instigate 'feeds' enables information-sharing with others. The more feeds, the more robust the information base and so the greater the 'stickiness' of the site. Concurrently the business enjoys network effects, that is the value to each user grows as users use the site.

Ultimately, not only do product boundaries extend in digitised contexts but so too do the boundaries of what comprises the customer. In the digital economy, fluid organisations are accompanied by fluid products and fluid customers. Like Amazon.com, Facebook.com delivers online advertising to users based on their activities. Users can give adverts 'thumbs-up' or 'thumbs-down', which focuses the 'permission marketing' dimension of Facebook.com. This thereby further enhances its stickiness. Such a digital product, which rests on consumer input for its design and which continuously changes, has to translate into a viable business model that is ultimately profitable. Pricing might be seen as key to enabling this. If users' interactions themselves become the product for advertisers, then the marketing platform must be priced competitively *vis-à-vis* alternatives for advertisements. The product in terms of interactions is dissociated from the pricing in operational terms. The costs of enabling interactions must accord with profits but not necessarily with pricing. Consumer interactions are not charged to customers by Facebook.com yet they are resource-intense. Their zero price is at odds with the cost of their provision. Revenue generation capacity via advertising rests on this premise.

The possibility of 'co-creation' between companies and consumers alters certain fundamental aspects of the traditionally perceived link between costs, pricing, profits and the product. Most enterprises have a developed architecture which cannot capitalise on co-creation. Their design focuses on the processes which create the products and services, and the assumption is that producers should manage owned resources. In the digital economy, this assumption will not tally with the new realities of the economics of production, consumption, pricing and profits. Investments in IT may, within a web-enabled company, be key to driving the co-creation process, which is the ultimate source of profitability. Fixed costs, such as those of IT, are the most difficult to relate directly to prices because they need to be allocated first, which is dependent on units sold, and which itself is reflective of price charged.

In the context of internet technologies, many IT costs will be not just fixed but also sunk because of IT infrastructure specificity and because of the applications software development costs which are specific to the specific IT application. Consequently such IT costs lead to pricing positions whereby volume of use becomes key to ultimate profitability. An expensive and highly capital-intensive web-based enterprise without users has little potential of achieving long-term viability. In the case of Facebook, or YouTube or Flickster or Googlemail, no price is attached to use of the site by consumers but the volume of users will ultimately attract advertisers willing to pay a price to engage the users' attention.

Success dependency on the volume of users of a web-based enterprise creates indirect links between investments enabling the production of services and the achievement of profits or economic viability. It is this lack of direct linkages which renders traditional pricing approaches partly inadequate for digitised firms. Digitisation is one dimension of the arguments related to altering cost management and pricing approaches. But it is the changing structure that underpins digitisation which offers scope for novel business cost behaviours and relationships. One key source of altered organisational digital practice is cloud computing.

4.5 Cloud Costing

Recently the CEO of Google, Eric Schmidt, predicted that in the very near future 90% of the computing delivered through desktop PCs today will be handled in the 'cloud' by remote servers (*Information Age*, December 2008, p. 50). Cloud computing refers to software that does not need to be downloaded. Historically, computer hardware came with built-in software in terms of both systems and applications. Subsequently, software was decoupled from hardware, and applications also became separated from the operating system. Additionally, the user interface became detached from applications and, under virtualisation, operating systems can today be dissociated from hardware. So the remote delivery of computing as a scaleable service without the need for re-installing – which hides the complexity of computing from the user – is another step in the growing flexibility of organisational resources. A cloud service has three distinct characteristics that differentiate it from traditional approaches to accessing computing services. It is sold on demand, usually in relation to time period of usage. The user can determine extent of usage which makes it elastic. Additionally, the 'cloud' is managed by the provider. Extensive innovations in virtualisation and distributed computing, as well as improved access to high-speed internet and a weak economy, have accelerated the growth of cloud computing. What is of significance here is the ability of support systems to shift from exhibiting high long-term fixed costs to lower fixed costs and ultimately to entirely transforming cost behaviour characteristics. Control over time and extent of usage and the non-incurrence of costs associated with operating an in-house IT service relating to what can be 'clouded' allow the potential of shifting and altering cost structures. The scalability of cloud-based systems on the part of service providers reduces the implementation, running and maintenance costs to enterprises. Both its product – in terms of information output for managerial use – and its operational premise alter the underlying cost incursions as well as assumptions and therefore require the rethinking of management accounting information for allocation and decision purposes.

The implications for management accounting are significant. At one level, informational and computing services that are the most current and advanced become readily available to all organisations – large and small. Consequently computing resources become commoditised and do not endow differentiating appeal to firms. However their usage can continue to demarcate corporate success. The 1980s and 1990s made evident that operational effectiveness and efficiency can be undermined by incorrect costing information, and indicated that many managers regarded information processing as key to organisational success. This was a time of growing production complexity in manufacturing and service environments, as well as increased diversity in terms of product offerings. It was also a time of increased investments in fixed costs by firms to allow flexibility and market competitiveness as well as coupled direct cost incursions. This made unit product-based allocations more difficult and problematic than in the past – so much so that cost allocation and cost management approaches began to be viewed as core competitive competencies.

In the same sense the use to which information is put, rather than its availability, will enable some firms to extract economic gains better than others. Advances such as cloud computing will render all organisations information-intense at low cost and in a technologically adept and modern manner. Information access under such circumstances becomes essential for cost management awareness, but decision effectiveness will continue to rely on the intelligent use of information. Management accounting professionals will need to heed the ease of access to information alongside change in its provenance and its relationship to production and customer processes. They will in much more complex contexts seek to maintain legitimacy as purveyors of financial information in a decision-useful and ready form.

4.6   The Strategic Scorecard

The notion that 'balance' in information output is essential in the compilation and production of management accounting information was popularised during the 1990s. This was an important and key argument in the purveyance of the balanced scorecard (BSC) (Kaplan and Norton, 1992). It has since become evident that both the content and the organisation of the BSC are considered to affect managerial judgment (Lipe and Salterio, 2002). The CIMA Strategic Scorecard™ was developed in response to the important findings that emerged from a project led by IFAC and CIMA to develop a framework of enterprise gover-nance. The idea of balance that is posited in the 'balanced' scorecard was thereby elevated to the realm of the board of directors. Boards of companies have, since the 1990s, increasingly been subjected to scrutiny in terms of aligning strategic objectives with corporate conformance requirement as a stewardship obligation. This led to concern with enterprise governance, which refers to the set of responsibilities and practices exercised by boards and executive managers with the aim of providing strategic direction, ensuring that objectives are achieved, ascertaining that risks are managed appropriately and verifying that the organisation's resources are used responsibly. The frame of reference rests on distinguishing conformance with corporate governance requirements from the drive to derive performance from such adherence. Figure 4.1 captures the distinction.

The conformance dimension deals with issues such as board structures and roles, and executive remuneration. Codes and/or standards generally address this dimension with some compliance being subject to the assurance of audit verification.

Enterprise governance	
Conformance (corporate governance processes)	Performance (business governance processes)
Chairman/CEO	Strategic planning and alignment
Non-executive directors	Strategic decision making
Audit committee	Scorecards
Resources and remuneration committee	Strategic enterprise systems
Strategic risk management for compliance	Continuous improvement
Controls assurance	Strategic risk management
Accountability assurance	Value creation/resource utilisation

Figure 4.1 The Enterprise Governance Framework.
(*Source*: CIMA Strategic Scorecard (CIMA, 2007)).

Approaches for the conformance dimension exist to assess their effective operation. Well-established oversight mechanisms can be put into place by the board to ensure that good corporate governance processes are proving effective. Committees composed mainly or wholly of independent non-executive directors can prove effective, and audit committees or their equivalent in other contexts can also be used. Other approaches to conformance include nominations committees and remuneration committees.

The performance dimension focuses on strategy and value creation. The aim is to aid the board to make strategic decisions, assess its attitude to risk and recognise the primary drivers of performance. This dimension cannot readily be subjected to audit, but the CIMA Strategic Scorecard™ is an approach that can be implemented across different types of organisation as a relevant tool for signalling and monitoring strategic pursuits and their alignment to desired performance (CIMA, 2007).

CIMA considers that good corporate governance can possibly assist in averting failure, but naturally it cannot assure good business performance. Attention to performance levels attained in terms of strategic decision making and implementation has not, up to now, been a board-level priority. CIMA views the enterprise governance framework as possibly assisting in clarifying both conformance and performance in terms of the organisation's long-term success.

But even though strategy may be regarded as the responsibility of the board, no specific oversight mechanisms for it that are comparable to the audit committee are evident in practice. Issues such as remuneration or financial reporting may be put under scrutiny by a dedicated board committee of independent non-executive directors and referred back to the full board, but strategy does not receive the same attention and comparable scrutiny mechanisms do not exist. The responsibility generally lies with the entire board. CIMA considers this an oversight gap in relation to strategy. Perhaps the level of discretion over judgments concerning the appropriateness of

the idea for the product underpinned decision making, which then influenced wider enterprise possibilities.

In 2008, the US government's decision not to bail out Lehman Brothers touched off an unexpected chain of events which made an already uncertain business environment profoundly uncertain. The government's reasoning was that the company was not financially as big as other firms which had been rescued. Economic analysis coupled with political concerns to avoid moral hazard seemed to drive the decision. The repercussions were global and wide-ranging (Bryan and Farrell, 2009). In a financial world tied together by an intricate web of dependencies among financial institutions and industrial organisations, the unexpected collapse of a long-established market player like Lehman Brothers led to an unmitigated shock of global proportion. Over the subsequent 6 months, financial collapses and economic failures saw the loss of global net worth reach $30 trillion, and a $10 trillion policy package by governments internationally was the initial response. Commentators noted that earlier rescue packages for failing financial institutions had 'introduced massive moral hazard into the markets, allowing investment banking executives and their boards to believe that they wouldn't be allowed to fail' (John Carney, *Clusterstock. com*, 29/12/2008). The US government's response was unexpected. Its blend of economic and political analysis led to a decision with far-reaching and, to a large degree, unexpected consequences.

Decisions focusing on costs and benefits bring unintended consequences. They have, in the history of organisational functioning and institutional operations, always had effects beyond the realm of the analyses that took place at the time of the decisions. Increasingly, significant decisions by large organisations have to take heed of wide level factors engaging analysis of risk, governance, regulation and political, strategic and financial concerns which all encompass global rather than just domestic factors. Decisions have become more complex and their consequences, whether anticipated or not, take less time to make an impact. Today the consequences of financially based decisions have to co-mingle with non-financial considerations, and their related actions have wide-reaching and sometimes global repercussions. Decision making of the global impact variety is subject to alterations in the timeframe in which effects get shaped. The speed and level of impact is often cyclical. There are many historical examples of dynamic and integrated global growth which ended in eruptions of financial instability and geo-political disorder. For instance, the French and British empires of the 18th century were of global proportion. They disintegrated into military, social and economic chaos after the Napoleonic Wars and the American Revolution, respectively. The integrated nature of the institutional societal structures of the 19th century collapsed after the First World War and the crisis of the Great Depression (James, H, *McKinseydigital.com*, 26/3/09). The contention is that every globalisation up-swing is driven by technical advances which run ahead of the capacity of institutions to devise adjustment mechanisms. The recent spate of technological innovations has yet to make a full adaptive impact within organisations. Control mechanisms, including management accounting, still lag technological change.

Financial transactions, which are deemed to provide foundations for the measurement of the value of goods, are dependent on stable financial systems. When these break down, a crisis in valuation and cost–benefit analysis ensues. Decision making then stops relying entirely on fundamentals and so unco-ordinated, impulsive and potentially ineffective decisions get made. Up-swings and down-turns will occur more rapidly as the global economy integrates because effects and consequences spread more swiftly. This is the context in which management accounting presently operates. The management accountant must today deal with enabling sound decision making in the face of extreme crises which come and go at an accelerating pace.

4.8   Regulation in a Risky World

In a world afflicted by financial instability, governments as well as global institutions seek to create order, stability and certainty. In the near term, the impact of this is likely to be that enterprises will operate in a global context where governments assume an expanded role in financial markets. A rise in regulation will affect international enterprise activities in both the service and the manufacturing sectors. Calls are being made for the re-regulation of financial institutions and global capital markets. In the UK, the Financial Services Authority has proposed wide-ranging macro- and micro-regulatory changes which will impact on the workings of not just financial institutions but also the financial management of the organisations they service. The Bank for International Settlements has likewise proposed enhancements to the 'Basel II' framework which regulates financial institutions' capital requirements and securitisation, and stipulates capital constraints. The approach to financial risk management is both set to become more formulaic while at the same time allowing more discretion to enable adherence to regulation, both in letter and in spirit.

The International Accounting Standards Board (IASB) and the US's Financial Accounting Standards Board (FASB) are also committed to jointly determining appropriate steps in the face of the financial crisis, to achieve the aim of effectively converging International Financial Reporting Standards (IFRSs) and US GAAP. The setting up by them of the Financial Crisis Advisory Group is intended to enable the boards to be guided in this task by appealing to the expertise of global investors, regulators, central banks, finance markets and policy-makers. In this regard, the IASB Chairman, David Tweedie, has noted the desire for 'standard setters to seek global solutions to a global crisis' (www.iasb.org, 24/3/09), and the Chairman of the FASB, Robert Herz, has affirmed the value of working to develop 'common responses to reporting issues from the global financial crisis' (*ibid*). The uncertainty of idiosyncratic and nation-specific approaches to financial management and risk regulation is institutionally widely regarded as an impediment to decision making in a global economy. In regulatory environments which increasingly operate in standardised forms, transparency is viewed as enhanced due to the perceived comfort of commonality of approach to measurement, valuation and financial representation. In such a world, the management accountant's task is two-fold: to understand the requirements to represent economic flows in a manner that is reconcilable with the external demands on the organisation of global uniformity and, more importantly, to seek out whether formally required standardised representations of performance and activities of other firms with which interactions are or may take place – whether local or global – have organisation-specific elements which may materially affect financial decisions. In essence, inhabiting a globalised organisational environment requires management accountants to develop the ability to function effectively and adeptly with standardised, converging representations of economic flows in an intelligent manner.

What remains largely uncertain is how far governments, policy-setting institutions and regulatory bodies will succeed in developing standardised regulatory, trade, fiscal and monetary frameworks. We also do not know how areas such as the economic role of government and financial institutions, and the rise of new business models, will – in a regulated and converging world – maintain differences and distinctiveness. Thus the management accounting profession is entering an era of growing complexity, not just (as in the past) focused on organisational or industrial changes, but one that has a global span of effects. In a world of growing complexity and uncertainty where it is sought that economic representations become standard, coherent and convergent, the ability to assess alternative scenarios, to consider their implications and to take corresponding action will determine financial viability. The traditional foundations of management accounting will, in such an environment, be extensively tested.

Chapter 5

The Rising Tide of Change in Management Accounting

5.1 Introduction

Many issues have emerged recently which are of concern both to managers relying on financial management information and to management accounting thinkers, practitioners and professional institutes. The growth of strategic issues has been, and continues to be, a focal point of attention. Advances in information systems and internet-based technologies are of importance also. Environmental sustainability in management (Soonawalla, 2006) and innovation (Cooper and Slagmulder, 2006) will likely alter management accounting practice in the near term. Forces of globalisation and the worldwide financial crisis which began in 2008 have also led to novel insights relating to managerial practices and decisions. But aside from these effects, enterprises are seeing various changes which will impact on management even further. These can be expected to affect management control practices and management accounting in a transformational manner.

In previous chapters we have discussed technological changes, digitisation and strategic issues in relation to management accounting. Our focus here is to consider their interaction alongside other factors impinging on management accounting. We consider in particular the issue of globalisation and collaborative alliances, the rise of virtual organisations as a special case of fluid structuring, and other enterprise-related effects which have caused a fusion of issues to begin to impact the field – and which will bring into question many of the assumptions that prevail about management accounting expertise and knowledge.

5.2 Questioning Management Accounting's *Raison d'être*

Until recently many management commentators discussed globalisation in the context of debates about the merits and drawbacks of outsourcing and off-shoring.

The rationale initially was articulated in terms of the value to enterprises of outsourcing support activities like payroll, tax, IT services and the manufacture of subcomponents. But some firms quickly moved to outsourcing core activities such as design, innovation, research and customer relationship management. And management accountants were brought in within many firms to take a closer look. Today, the debate is no longer over demarcating which type of activities firms should consider outsourcing but has focused on whether, for some firms, outsourcing allows the variabilising of fixed costs, and whether there are economies of scale and value returns from doing so.

In some organisations the question has been whether there are risks which, in the longer term, need to be assessed and compared to short-term cost containment or savings. What is evident is that rapid shifts cause traditional approaches to controlling enterprise resources to be questioned. For instance relatively high oil prices in the last quarter of 2008 were followed by reductions in prices by two-thirds in the subsequent quarter, and this brought to light the fact that many decisions were made in 2008 on the premise that change is part of everyday life for organisations but without full acknowledgment of the extreme pace of volatility. This is a very recent phenomenon which has caught many firms off-guard. Extrapolating expectations of change into the future is no longer sufficient. The acceleration of volatility, and the uncertainty over volatility itself, are today of real concern to managers. Thus when oil prices well exceeded US$100 a barrel, the merits of off-shoring were being questioned by some firms because the cost of freight movement and supply management stretched resources, and they moved in favour of domestic production. But the argument could not be sustained for very long, and many decisions – which led to erroneous long-term investments based on an expectation of less volatility, less dynamic processes and slower shifting standard variances – were engaged in adversely.

Risk management has, like globalisation, become an issue of principal concern to organisations. The difficulty is that we have entered a world not just of growing uncertainty and economic vicissitudes, but also of rapid acceleration in the pace of change. When the timing of decisions becomes of extreme importance, the luxury of being able to delay long-term decisions to allow for uncertainty resolution is no longer available. What is clear is that not only do enterprises tend to focus more on economic calculative practices to a greater extent than before, but also during economic downturns they are prone to develop tighter costing controls. Two consequences of this are that management accounting will face pressures for 'knee-jerk' reactions based on past responses while at the same time it will have the opportunity to react to the growing sense of risk and its consequences and to offer new insights.

Many issues today reflect novel business decisions where traditional problems become complex as a result of new conditions, and in response answers are expected from management accounting and from analytical insight. The combination of extensive financial volatility, rapid technological change and the impacts of the forces of globalisation has produced a climate of extreme change and risk, but also brings opportunities for management and the management accounting field to act in innovative and thoughtful ways.

There are today entirely novel business models and forms of enterprise functioning which are re-shaping modes of management accounting operationalisation. Different styles of accounting for risk are emerging (Mikes, 2009). The rise of fluid organisations is changing the type and scope of information exchanges within and across firms, and is altering the very definition of what constitutes an enterprise. What gets represented in management accounting terms becomes as significant as the depth to which information now has to be reported to different parties. In this sense, strategic attention to costing knowledge is starting to underlie the politics of information communication in ways that have not been anticipated.

Further, products themselves in the digital economy exhibit shifting boundaries. Purchasing a product on eBay can for some consumers be as much about the purchase experience as about product ownership. And while product boundaries are now more malleable, so too are consumers more fluid in that producers and consumers are often no longer categorically separable. This fosters attention towards pricing, costing and profit-making issues as well as towards new and different contingencies. Although it has long been recognised that simplified representations of cost relationships were never entirely suitable for achieving effective cost management in firms, they are today even less so. In some enterprises customers may be producers, not paying for goods or services consumed, and revenue generation may be dissociated from customer-generated transactions but may still be dependent on customers. In such complex market environments, management accounting must alter its vision.

In relation to quantitative representations, accounting has always been extensively numbers-based and financial. Indeed it is this that has separated accounting from other forms of information provision. Quantification has dominated in guiding managerial activities in the industrial economy. How far this will continue in a more complex economy focusing on the production of knowledge goods and the creation of products which allow customers to customise is a new question for management accounting. Where management accounting at present selectively simplifies cost and resource relationships to enable quantified analysis (see Chapter 2), the *status quo* may have to give way to new contingencies driven by complexity, as well as to the need for greater transparency. As such, quantification will take new forms. It may involve addressing many more issues which are still the realm of qualitative information and it will drive the integration of many information sources in attempts to grasp the implications of organisational changes. Moreover, it will be sought that quantified reasoning will find novel ways of blending with non-calculative assessments of managerial and organisational situations.

The assumption has always been made that management accounting information is produced to satisfy the decision making needs of managers, which necessitate particular information. Grounded in this notion is the idea that managers analyse the information to which they have access and subsequently mobilise action following decisions. This idealised conception of the managerial process is one which has always guided management accounting information production, and is one which has been prescribed in rationales about the profession's *raison d'être*. But such a view may not represent the reality of all organisational processes, or at least there may be alternate views which may be taken of managerial modes of operation.

In some contexts, the formal evaluation of information may not precede managerial action. Action may simply be subsumed in assessments of information. Or action may sometimes be taken on the basis of non-formal information assessment, and the deployment of rational information may follow rather than lead decision implementation because of a prescribed expectation that formal evaluation before acting has to be legitimated through representations of rationality. The ways in which fast-paced change in management contexts is taking place have the potential greatly to shape the role of the management accountant as information producer and provider.

Historically it is the case that, with the advent of privileged economistic conceptions of organisational activities, quantification went hand-in-hand with responsible management. Management accounting then echoed this and focused on quantitative representations of organisational activities – the field followed the organisational actors who followed the numbers. And then, as it became paramount for management accountants to contribute to strategic concerns, management accounting followed the perceived needs of actors within firms who sought to be more strategic. Subsequently, management accounting followed the actors who wanted to focus on non-financials and narrative reports. After this, the field sought to follow the actors who wanted to be more market-adept. Today, organisational actors perceive a need for their activities to be made more visible, more transparent and more penetrable by regulation. So management accounting is becoming more concerned with risk assessment, governance mechanisms and the enablement of company directors to understand corporate strategic management from a wider stakeholder and stewardship viewpoint, rather than a pure and narrowly defined shareholder perspective. These are issues which will, in the near future, be of concern to the field.

5.3   The End of Traditionally Separate Entities

Some management accounting commentators have suggested that the field of management accounting did not see great alterations from the 1920s until the late 1970s when Far East countries' competition overwhelmed many Western firms (Johnson and Kaplan, 1987). Others contest this view (Ezzamel *et al.*, 1990). The field nevertheless moved to adopt a series of novel approaches designed to cope with these challenges during the 1980s (Bromwich and Bhimani, 1994). As argued in this book, it is likely that during the next decade rapid changes in technology, the globalisation of business activities and the extreme financial turmoil being witnessed in many markets, plus the concerns with risk and global governance, will usher in a wave of calls for further changes in the field.

We have noted that advances in information technology and digitisation have created new relationships between and across enterprise processes. Information technology and web-based exchanges are increasingly extensive across firms and are becoming central to their economic activities. The term 'digital economy' has been coined to represent:

> *...the pervasive use of IT (hardware, software, application and telecommunication) in all aspects of the economy, including internal operations of organisations (business, government and non-profit); and transactions between individuals, acting both as consumers and citizens, and organisations.*

> *Atkinson and McKay (2007, p. 7).*

Communication technologies – including the telegraph, radio and television – have, over much of the past century, evolved very rapidly in terms of functionality, capacity and features, and have often done so independently of computer technologies. Mobile telephony has further changed the shape of interfacing and information exchange in almost unbounded ways. Computers (especially personal computers) have, since their initial availability in the 1940s, developed at so fast a pace as to now affect the lives of essentially every organisational participant. Another industry which has seen extensive re-shaping over the past century is that of media and entertainment. As distinct industries, what has been achieved by communication and computer technologies, alongside the transformation of media and entertainment as well as the software industry, has been very wide-reaching. But importantly the emergence of a digital economy could only come about through the convergence of previously distinct industries.

It is now impossible to envisage these industries outside the context of their merged potential. The internet could only achieve its large-scale impact because of the very extensive availability of computers and network technologies. This altered possibilities for media and commerce, enabling them to be fully 'electronified'. The ready presence of software applications and content enabled, and was in turn further enabled, by connectivity. IT systems and their *modus operandi* achieved continuous growth because of standardised connecting platforms and the near commoditisation of their individual modules, and they were fuelled by the co-ordination enabling capacity of networked IT systems. In essence digital convergence is at the core of the present day irreversibly networked environment, which has integrated and is further integrating previously distinct industries. Today the further conceptualisation of technological systems is undertaken on the premise that they must be networkable and subject to dynamic changes (Castells, 2001).

People can, in such a world, act while thinking how to act. Objectives here get defined by and within managerial action. Activities embed objectives. Objectives emerge during action rather than being decided prior to decisions (Bhimani and Bromwich, 2009). The digital age is an enmeshed world of inter-penetrating digital devices that re-shape all areas of economic activity. Financial control and management accounting activities as part of the digital economy are being altered, are integrating decision making and action, and are re-engineering the strategy, technology and cost information interface.

Within emerging organisational structures in today's economy, the idea that strategic decisions should be premised on categorical dissociation from action may be misguided. The advent of digitisation and its attendant consequences for the convergence of industries, as discussed above, suggest that businesses cannot extract all technological or operational choices from their strategic decision-making processes.

Management theorists and commentators presume generally that decision-making activities and managerial action are and should be sequential. Certainly during the early 1990s much effort was placed on developing a 'scientific' notion of management whereby some organisational participants think and others engage in action (Drori and Meyer, 2006). In many ways this presumption continues in that the doing of things is regarded as an activity that is purposefully distinct from the defining of desired activities to be executed. Just as calculation is keenly viewed as a legitimate domain of accounting in spite of the different approaches to understanding its operation in enterprises (Mennicken, 2002), so, this line of thinking – about objectives followed by and distinguished from action – is also an integral essence of prescribed approaches to the management function (Mintzberg, 1989) including management accounting.

Financial managers and accountants are being encouraged to be more strategic, which assumes objectives precede action. This is in part related to professional management accountancy bodies embracing a more strategic posture for their expertise and seeking to encourage strategic thinking in the practice of financial and cost management. This is not to say that management accountancy promotes the maintenance of a traditional staff instead of line role for accountants in practice, but that strategy is conceptualised in prescriptive terms as an activity dissociated from operation though preceding it. Many cost management approaches, including activity-based management, product life-cycle costing, target cost management, customer profitability analyses and strategic investment appraisal among others, have been predicated on the idea that strategic thinking should direct managerial action (Bhimani, 2009a).

The meshing of strategic, technological and operational decisions is indicative of a need to reformulate management accounting precepts across some areas. An important point of departure is to explore, within different contexts, the applicability of the premise that action follows structured cogitation and analysis and the actual use of management accounting information in novel organisational settings (Hopwood, 1983).

The shift towards converging industries across many economic markets, and the co-mingling of strategic, technological and operational decisions within many new organisations within these markets, make it desirable to investigate both what constitutes managerially useful information and the idea that strategic intent, technological options and management accounting information usage are distinct categories that are separable from one another and that adhere to a sequential path. What constitutes relevant information, and the presumed sequence of its deployment in organisationally networked contexts, may now need to be rethought. Just as convergence among previously distinct and independent industries has integrated pursuit and action and, perhaps, decision making and process, so management accounting may not retain its present significance without exploration of alternative modes of existence.

Financial information relevance is today more about the effective representation of strategic and technological inter-dependencies enabling managerial decisions to align with contemporary organisational action. Enterprises which depart from the conventional industrial model often fuse strategic and financial considerations. Their inter-relationships make it difficult for management accounting to prevail in a world of assumed reporting entry points at pre-defined structural nodes. Financial control and management information is becoming integral to, and immanent within, assessments of operational, strategic and cost considerations. Collaborative firm linkages and virtual enterprises represent extensive possibilities as arenas of management accounting change and innovation. Some possible implications of organisational forms along these lines for management accounting are discussed below.

▌ 5.4   Cross-organisational Exchanges

The 'make-or-buy' decision for an enterprise requiring components is one to which management accounting is regarded as being able to contribute. Conceptually, the costs and benefits accruing to a firm producing required parts or sub-components or carrying out a process internally are assessed versus the financial and managerial implications of outsourcing to external suppliers. Incremental cost analysis has been advocated as appropriate in helping to assess the financial consequences of managerial decisions. Traditionally, two options exist for a company wanting to buy a sub-component or a service-based product from an external supplier. The first option is for the buyer to put out a detailed bid for tender and choose the most competitive quote for a certain number of parts over a period of time or for certain quantities of services. Little attempt here is made to learn from past performance; exchanges tend to be at arm's length and to product specifications, and prices are well defined. This process is required by many public sector bodies. In contrast to this traditional 'transaction-based' competitive bidding approach, the buyer can establish a collaborative relationship (CR) with a supplier. Such a relationship would entail sharing of technical and financial information, managerial interaction and liaison, and a more flexible buyer–supplier link as to time/volume variables and product specifications. The costs involved in identifying the right supplier for a CR and operationalising such a link differ from those in a bidding situation. Firms regard one or the other approach as a strategic issue.

Competitive purchasing entails the assessment of certain economic transactions whose terms are made explicit prior to the commencement of trading. Agreements are put into place to cover recourse options for faltering or failing on the terms of the contract, and the buyer–supplier link is designed within attempts to minimise each party's dependence on the other. Conversely, collaborative sub-contracting relationships are founded on trust and transactional dependence with specific supply undertakings extending over only part of the overall trading relationship (Sako, 1992). The obligations of such long-term relationships are informal and changeable. The resolution of specific transaction problems on a case-by-case basis usually takes place through informal channels. The collaborative link exhibits mutual indebtedness that can extend over long periods of time governed by a loose principle of 'give and take'. A pure 'buy' situation is characterised by narrow and formal channels of communication between the buyer's purchasing department and the supplier's sales department, whereas a CR tends to have extensive and multiple channels of communication between a variety of functional managers and departments within the two companies. Another significant difference between a pure purchase and a collaborative linkage is that the latter establishes non-specific terms of trade as to supply quantity, timing of supply, product specifications and product price at the time of establishing the trading relationship. The buyer's ability to alter quantities purchased from the supplier and to change product specifications confers operational flexibility. An alliance such as this creates the possibility of rapid expansion and growth in ways that are not anticipated at the outset.

In broad terms the decision to enter into a CR with a supplier as opposed to engaging in transaction-focused pure purchase for required products entails a variety of organisational consequences with cost–benefit implications that stem from the various options affordable by the alliance. For instance, a CR allows the buyer to alter product specifications mid-stream depending on the volatility of market demands or competitive actions. To a degree this is also possible in virtual organisational set-ups if quantities for processing are contractually kept very low and continuously re-defined. Unplanned purchase volume changes, including temporary suspension of purchases, can be made throughout the term of the buying relationship. Further, the alliance relationship may lead to growth opportunities contingent upon entering the initial contract but not pre-defined at the time of its creation. Nevertheless there has to be an infra-structure and a sentiment to share operational information, including accounting information, between the trading partners.

Strategy, technology and costs as noted above are co-mingled within many modern organisational contexts. Managerial action and reactions are also becoming intertwined within the controls which must confront such co-mingling. Virtual firms engage very extensively in co-ordinating the purchase of products and services. The virtual firm can be viewed as an agglomeration of multiple 'buy' transactions that are weaved together by extensive managerial action, co-ordination and structuring. Cost analyses are likely to entail many factors reflective of the complexities such an agglomeration brings together.

A virtual enterprise has been defined as:

... a temporary network of independent companies – suppliers, customers and even rivals – linked by information technology to share skills, costs and access to one another's markets. This corporate model is fluid and flexible.

Byrne et al. (1993, p. 36).

Stress has been placed on viewing a virtual enterprise as a goal-orientated arrangement between several firms, or a unit within a firm which temporarily assembles competencies and capabilities wherever they arise. As Child *et al.* (2005, p. 168) note, a virtual organisation is effectively 'a repertoire of variable connectable modules built on an electronic information network' with each linked firm's function being to deliver a specific standardised product or service prior to decoupling. The intent is to create a flexible organisation of companies which become inter-locked for short time periods whereby each undertakes one or more functions.

Virtuality suggests temporary connections between otherwise independent entities via appropriate technological structures. Of particular importance is that this organisational form raises the issue of whether managerial structures are differentiated from virtual firms in terms of managerial imperatives: a characterising feature of virtual organisations is the commoditisation of information to enhance flexibility and 'infinite switching capacity', so that 'by reducing dependency on the human being as the bearer of knowledge and skill, it is possible to increase the flexibility of decision making and control to unprecedented levels' (Mowshowitz, 1994, p. 281). There may be standardisation of interaction whereby enterprises can be readily coupled and de-coupled, and new linkages created and dissolved, as the need for altered supply arises. This may then necessitate the codification and standardisation of information to provide a basis for control information to align across firms.

A virtual enterprise will have overhead costs arising from the running of its information system structure and carrying out co-ordination processes. Overhead costs will reflect remuneration of employees which may be a function partially of co-ordination effectiveness. A virtual corporation cannot always take advantage of scale and scope economies because of the autonomous structure of its component units. It will search for value creation through co-ordination structures rather than by reducing the costs of material input or services. Trust security measures are essential and potentially costly due to the risk of information leakage and opportunistic behaviour by engaging parties. Within virtual corporations, little room exists for tapping into organisational learning as information exchange for data build-up is not an aim across the agglomeration of entities.

Managerial emphasis within virtual enterprises is placed on effective and swift information processing and the co-ordination of individuals and connecting firms. Priorities must be quickly communicated to parties without the necessary investments for organisational culture generation. Managerial focus is on the management of people, co-ordination activities and the application of technology. The ultimate objective is the effective management of integral supply chains, fast response to competitors' actions, and shorter time to bring products to market. Effects such as these must be brought about in the absence of high face-to-face contacts.

A significant issue of control is that virtual organisations are focused less on controlling how work is undertaken and more on the outcomes of work. An enterprise which has developed its own hierarchy to carry out activities will be highly vertically integrated and centralised. Its in-sourcing activities will need close operational controls and it will affect tight involvement with physical processes. By direct contrast a virtual firm maintains arm's length transactions focused on short-term exchanges between electronically linked organisations. The focus will be on co-ordination rather than ownership of physical assets and on operating as an 'intellectual holding company' (Straub, 2004, p. 300).

Individual firms carrying out operational activities will invest in process controls based perhaps on standard costing analysis and established budgetary controls tied to operating plans and activities. Their focus will rest on performance monitors of their output. The virtual trading firm will stress outcome controls. Virtual firms are less operationally process control-orientated, evaluating instead performance monitors reflecting outcomes. The ability to monitor outsourced processes via outcome controls is, for a virtual firm, a relevant core competency. Where integrated activities prevail, an enterprise controls its processes via some equity in production activities. A virtual firm by contrast will not keep an equity position in other activities but will develop core resource for effective co-ordination and service delivery via more extensive outcome-based performance controls. The rise of virtual enterprises thus engenders the need for parallel management accounting approaches.

Focusing on controlling outcomes in the absence of an equity stake requires altered monitors relating to costs and resource allocation and movement. In some instances, dis-engagement from owning resources and emphasising co-ordination can be accompanied by a tilt towards variable costs and a lower fixed cost base. Where the disadvantages of scope and scale economies facing virtual firms can be overcome, reductions in both fixed and variable costs can accrue. Larger virtual firms can become larger if their ability to tap into scale effects is synthesised.

In broad terms, the complexities of globalisation combined with the rise of digitally-enabled enterprise forms within fast-changing markets generate new possibilities for management accounting which necessitate the need to alter, at least in part, the focused nature of its knowledge base. As noted, the managerial adaptation of coupling decision-making thinking with action has implications for management accounting-based controls. Standardised and electronic transactions embed both decisions and actions. Moreover, the rise of web-based business models and indeed virtual organisational forms bring to the fore novel accounting control requisites.

5.4.1   Accountants as Business Partners

One way forward for management accounting to contribute in a world of change is to seek to be seen as 'business partners' with other functions in the organisation. Throughout this book it has been indicated that most of the responses to change originated outside the accounting area. Thus flexible and fluid firms rely on, among others, teams of engineers, logistics designers, product planners and information systems, personnel specialists and lawyers. This is also true of designing for the customer and for generally global markets, and of customising 'global products' for individual countries. Here, additionally, marketing and corporate planning are involved.

Similarly, flexible organisations in terms of virtual organisations involve teams including engineers, purchasing officers, corporate planners, lawyers, information technologists and corporate governance specialists. Additionally, divisional managers and their teams are being given greater delegated power in many firms. Of course traditionally organised accountants are involved in all these endeavours, especially in generating cost information and in investment appraisal. However, the often centralised position of accountants, and their stewardship and monitoring roles, inhibit their contribution to such teams in ways suggested in this and early chapters. Often this means that costs and investment are downgraded in importance in reaching decisions. For management accountants to play their key role in decision making in all these staff areas, it may be desirable in some firms to 'embed' management accountants in the organisational teams as providers of the financial and other information 'owned' by the finance function but tailored to the needs of the team. They would be, as financial advisers, partners sharing the team's goals and being clearly within the team and located in its territory.

Many large firms are experimenting with freeing accountants from their existing 'silos' and establishing them as, at least, accounting ambassadors into other areas of the firm. Here management accountants help other managers by both performing the management accounting tasks of the team to which they are attached, sometimes called 'hybrid' accountants (Burns and Baldvinsdottir, 2005; Kurunmaki and Miller, 2006), indicating the finance division's perspective on decisions whilst also fulfilling stewardship, monitoring and compliance roles for the finance division. Thus many major endeavours by firms have implications for financial management. As ambassadors, accountants have a potentially strong line role in the management of complexity within firms given the ultimate linkages to issues of financial relevance and impact. But operational advances by management accountants willing to act in line capacities will take place alongside new reporting roles and expectations. For instance, the growth in governance, risk and environmental and sustainability concerns are today making demands on financial reporting. Here, the issues are complex entailing both a representational as well as a legitimating role. Organisations need to both report and inform on their activities as well as provide sound justifications for them (Hopwood, 2009). The finance function will thus be looked at to respond to such increasingly complex demands.

Some firms have gone further and allowed accountants as business partners to identify strongly with the team in which they are embedded and to act fully as the team's management accountant and financial adviser. From the finance division's perspective, a moral hazard problem may arise if the business partner over-identifies with the interests and objectives of the team. Thus objective regulation of the teams would have to be undertaken by the central staff of the finance division. For similar reasons, the line responsibility of the business partner may be obscure, as may be the career opportunities offered. Most firms are still seeking to clarify the relationship of business partners with the finance division and the team with which they are associated. This is a crucial challenge for a firm's top management if accounting is to achieve its full role in the firm.

5.5   Avenues of Change

This and prior chapters demonstrate the capacity for management accounting to change in the face of emerging concerns. Earlier chapters show that the field has exhibited this over a long period of time, seeking often to emerge with solutions to particular issues but with cognisance that new techniques operate in the context of behavioural, organisational, institutional and political dynamics. As a consequence it is widely accepted that techniques do not operate in isolation of such contextual dimensions and pursuits do not always achieve desired intent. But the value of the field continues to find form across many dimensions. The present is a time of immense change in which management accounting continues to be confronted by demands to achieve, react and pro-act in ways it has not been called upon before to do. This presents opportunities and challenges. The following identifies and summarises, from this and prior chapters, many of the pressures and potential considerations the field must address.

1. There is both accelerating uncertainty and growing uncertainty about volatility across enterprise environments. This means that assumptions, projections, prognostications and information analysis now take place with different expectations and objectives. It is the management accountant's obligation to assess the propriety of continuing with the *status quo*.

2. Many products are now produced in a manner which no longer follows the logic that was part of the traditional industrial era. An organisation conventionally invests in conceptualising, designing and testing a product prior to its production; marketing and sales functions then take charge of enabling customers access to the product. Today many industrial, service-based and digital products get created directly from customer input and design. In the case of electronic media, the content is generated by the consumers and adverts on the interactive platform between users form the revenue source. In these contexts pricing and costing issues do not follow a traditional model which may be cost-plus based or market-based. Rather the pricing has to tie in directly to the strategy of the firm along different parameters. The challenge is for management accountants to provide input into this process in a valuable manner.

3. A conventional assumption in management accounting systems design thinking is that managers think and consider information *prior* to making decisions and taking action. It may however be that, in many instances, action is subsumed *within* assessments of information. Also, non-formal information may be crucial in determining organisational endeavours. Information appeal is even often made *following* decisions as a legitimacy-endowing ritual. As enterprises operate in a context of fast change and extreme uncertainty, the structured logic presumed of information use and decision making will need to be re-considered by management accountants, as will the use of non-formal information and the role of legitimacy in information deployment.

4. Information systems in organisations are seeing signs of a 'pull' rather than a 'push' philosophy driven by information users. Thus rather than seeing the finance function as a purveyor of pre-determined and pre-defined accounting reports conveyed indiscriminately to managers, customised and user-designed

financial control information is coming to be seen as a growing capability, if not an essential one, to be fulfilled by management accountants.

5. The meshing of strategic, technological and operational decisions in many organisations may drive the need to re-formulate management accounting precepts across certain areas. The applicability of the premise that action follows structured cogitation and analysis of management accounting information will have to be re-visited under different business models and architectures.

6. Transparency and compliance with growing regulatory requirements will impinge on enterprises. Management accounting will have to address issues of risk management and the design and implementation of appropriate governance mechanisms. Additionally, the growing concerns with sustainable business practices and environmental concerns will make demands for effective record capture and reporting approaches.

7. To enable quantified analysis management accounting, at times, selectively simplifies cost and resource relationships. But as new contingencies – driven by complexity and the need to respond to new reporting challenges in this age of transparency – emerge, novel ways of quantification will be sought. Moreover, innovative ways of blending quantitative and qualitative information will have to be determined.

8. Regulatory environments increasingly operate in standardised forms. This is partly because transparency is regarded as being thus enhanced due to the preference for commonality of approach to measurement, valuation and financial representation. Consequently, the management accountant needs to comprehend the manner in which economic flows can effectively be represented in a manner that is reconcilable with external demands for global uniformity. In addition, however, the need exists to develop the ability to function adeptly with standardised, converging representations of economic flows. For the field this represents a new foray.

9. Part of firms' essential core strengths is increasingly the development of appropriate strategic financial management expertise to recognise market opportunities which can be harnessed with the use of flexible organisational technologies to mobilise manufacturing and service re-design and production. Production technologies that permit flexibility across corporate web-based systems place enhanced pressure on organisations to understand and manage costs across business-to-business boundaries. Such changes are making new demands on financial management systems in organisations across many industries and must be heeded by the management accounting profession.

10. One lesson from our brief historical survey is that accounting innovations seem to take a long time to be widely accepted. Thus standard costing and budgetary control took from their introduction in the late 1920s and early 1930s until the

late 1950s/early 1960s to become widespread in the UK. Similarly discounted cash-flow investment appraisal was well-publicised by the early 1960s but took around 20 years to reach 80% usage in large firms in the UK. More recent innovations have also taken rather a long time to achieve any general take-up. Thus activity-based costing has made progress only slowly from the late 1980s to achieve a very low take-up currently. Both the balanced scorecard and economic value management techniques were well-publicised by the mid-1990s but still have taken a considerable time to be accepted in a widespread way. It is evident that change and the adoption of innovations take time. This is not necessarily indicative of an undesirable lag. Rather, enterprises may purposefully resist rapid change which jeopardises mechanisms that are valuable but not recognised as formal rationalised systems. Resistance to change thus can have non-discursive intelligence embedded within the organisation.

Many techniques have a very brief experimental life, and those that are sustained may have a very different level of take-up – compare that of ABC and the BSC above. The level of application of successful innovations may differ between firms and industries. Thus most firms pursue the concept of shareholder value maximisation but the level of detailed application varies widely, with relatively few large firms linking incentives to economic value management performance measures. This may be because no organisation embeds and adopts any technique quite as conceptually imagined. Organisations ground contextuality to the workings of techniques.

11. Much of the book regards accounting as having become more flexible and fluid in the face of much greater volatility in many sections of the environment faced by firms. This would seem to require many changes to contemporary routine accounting reporting methods. It may be that much of the flexibility and fluidity that seems to be required by accounting is manifested in information provided for *ad hoc* decisions and for strategy-making. Given the politics of information provider roles in organisations, and the many efforts to professionalise different bodies of expertise tied to the organisational realm, it may be that if management accountants do not respond to – or are not allowed to respond to – the challenges reviewed in this book and elsewhere, others will attempt to fulfil these needs.

12. It has been argued that management accountants need to understand the technology of firms. Such an understanding is required if management accountants are to be accepted within decision-making teams in organisations, to aid in outsourcing, capital budgeting and the design of virtual organisations. It was suggested that technology determines the firm's cost function and that these structures are more complex than those ordinarily used and assumed by accountants. It was also suggested that accounting needs more explicitly to

allow for multi-product production. This requires an understanding of multi-product economies of scale and of economies of scope, plus the trade-offs between scale and scope economies. Scope economies arise from resources that are jointly used by cost objects, that is they can be shared at little or no cost. Accounting for this jointness is a major challenge for management accounting, especially as many environmental developments generate joint resources. Thus most information resources have elements of jointness. In the contemporary economy, the complexities of jointness of costs are increasing, which may require parallel investments in developing analytical frames of reference in response. As organisations become more knowledge-management orientated, the focus may turn to enhancing some notion of returns on people rather than simply on capital. This will lead to the creation of organisations that seek to adapt continuously and to evolve based on knowledge input. If traditional structures give way to fluid enterprise designs and organisational forms that rest on expertise and knowledge creation potential then the management accountant will have to respond by re-thinking control approaches.

13. The ability of management accountants to understand other areas of organisational functioning and other business models, and to integrate this emerging knowledge with the work, tasks and objectives of the changing management accounting function, will be key to the profession's survival. The field must continue to be adept in recognising the significance and nature of emerging change as it evolves.

References

Afuah, A., Tucci, C., 2003. Internet Business Models and Strategies. McGraw-Hill, New York.

Ahrens, T., Chapman, C.S., 2005. Management control systems and the crafting of strategy: a practice-based view. In: Chapman, C.S. (Ed.), Controlling Strategy – Management Accounting and Performance Measurement. Oxford University Press, New York, pp. 106–124.

Ahrens, T., Chapman, C.S., 2007. Management accounting as practice. Account. Org. Soc. 32, 1–27.

Al-Omiri, M., Drury, C., 2007. A survey of factors influencing the choice of product costing systems in UK organizations. Manag. Account. Res. 18, 399–424.

Anderson, M.C., Banker, R.D., Janakiraman, S.N., 1995. Are selling, general and administrative costs 'sticky'? J. Account. Res. 41 (1), 47–63.

Anderson, S.W., 2006. Managing costs and cost structure throughout the value chain: research on strategic cost management. In: Chapman, C., Hopwood, A.G., Shields, M.D. (Eds.), Handbook of Management Accounting Research, vol. 2. Elsevier, Oxford, pp. 481–506.

Anderson, S.W., Lanen, W.N., 2007. Understanding cost management: what can we learn from the evidence on 'sticky costs'? Working Paper, January. <http://ssrn.com/abstract=975135>.

Anthony, R.N., 1956. Management Accounting: Text and Cases. Irwin, Homewood.

ASAE, 1997. Re-engineering the finance function. Financial Management Symposium, May 23.

Atkinson, R., McKay, A., 2007. Digital prosperity. ITIF. <http://www.itif.org/files/digital_prosperity.pdf>.

Ax, L., Bjornenak, T., 2007. Management accounting innovations: origins and diffusion. In: Hopper, T., Northcott, D., Scapens, R. (Eds.), Issues in Management Accounting. Pearson, London, pp. 357–376.

Banker, R.D., Ou, C., Potter, G., 1997. The compensating impact of strategic cost drivers from the US banking industry. Working Paper.

Baumol, W., 1996. Predation and the logic of the average variable cost test. J. Law Econ. (April), 49–72.

Baumol, W.J., Panzar, J.C., Willig, R.D., 1988. Contestable Markets and the Theory of Industry Structure. Harcourt Brace Jovanovich, New York.

Baxter, J., Chua, W.F., 2006. Reframing management accounting practice: a diversity of approaches. In: Bhimani, A. (Ed.), Management Accounting: European Perspectives. Oxford University Press, Oxford, pp. 42–68.

Bettencourt, L., Ulwick, A.W., 2008. The customer-centred innovation map. Harvard Business Review. Harvard Business School Press, Boston.

Bhimani, A., 1996. Management accounting in the UK: reflections on research, practice and the profession. In: Bhimani, A. (Ed.), Management Accounting: European Perspectives. Oxford University Press, Oxford.

Bhimani, A., 2004. Cost Management System Design: Balance and Organizational Knowledge Journal of Cost Management 18 (2), 26–34.

Bhimani, A., 2008. Strategic Finance. Strategy Press, London.

Bhimani, A., 2009a. Handbook of Management Accounting. CCH, London.

Bhimani, A., 2009b. Risk management, corporate governance and management accounting: emerging contingencies. Manag. Account. Res. 20 (1), 2–5.

Bhimani, A., Bromwich, M., 2009. Management accounting at the interface of strategy, technology and cost information. In: Chapman, C., Cooper, D.J., Miller, P. (Eds.), Accounting, Organizations and Institutions, Oxford University Press, Oxford.

Bhimani, A., Keshvarz, H., 1999. British management accountants: strategically oriented? J. Cost Manag. 13 (2), 25–31.

Bhimani, A., Langfield-Smith, K., 2007. Structure, formality and the importance of financial and non-financial information in strategy development and implementation. Manag. Account. Res. 18, 3–31.

Bhimani, A., Ncube, M., Soonawalla, K., 2006. Intuition and real options-based investment appraisal: a cross-national study of financial executives. J. Appl. Manag. Account. Res. 4 (2), 11–34.

Bhimani, A., Gosselin, M., Okano, H., Ncube, M., 2007a. Activity based costing: how far have we come internationally? Cost Manag. 21 (3), 12–17.

Bhimani, A., Gosselin, M., Ncube, M., Soonawalla, K., 2007b. The value of accounting information in assessing investment risk. Cost Manag. 21 (1), 29–35.

Bhimani, A., Horngren, C.T., Datar, S., Foster, G., 2008. Management and Cost Accounting. FT/Prentice Hall, Hemel Hempstead.

Biddle, G.C., Steinberg, R.C., 1984. Allocation of joint and common costs. J. Account. Lit. 3, 1–45.

Bierman, S., Dyckman, T., 1971. Managerial Cost Accounting. Macmillan, New York.

Bierman, S., Smidt, S., 1960. The Capital Budgeting Decision. Macmillan, New York.

Bloch, M., Lempres, E.C., 2008. An interview with Filippo Passerini. McKinsey Quart. 4, 14–15.

Brierley, J.A., Cowton, C.J., Drury, C., 2001. Research into product costing practice: a European perspective. Eur. Account. Rev. 10 (2), 215–256.

Brierley, J.A., Cowton, C.J., Drury, C., 2007. Product costing practices in different manufacturing companies: a British survey. Int. J. Manag. 24 (4), 667–675.

Bromwich, M., 1990. The case for strategic management accounting: the role of accounting information for strategy in competitive markets. Account. Org. Soc. 15 (1–2), 27–46.

Bromwich, M., Bhimani, A., 1989. Management Accounting: Evolution Not Revolution. CIMA, London.

Bromwich, M., Bhimani, A., 1994. Management Accounting: Pathways to Progress. CIMA, London.

Bromwich, M., Hong, C., 1999. Activity-based costing systems and incremental costs. Manag. Account. Res. 10 (10), 39–60.

Bromwich, M., Hong, C., 2000. Costs and regulation in the UK telecommunications industry. Manag. Account. Res. 11, 137–165.

Bromwich, M., Walker, M., 1998. Residual income: past and future. Manag. Account. Res. 9, 39–419.

Bryan, L., Farrell, D., 2009. Leading through uncertainty. McKinsey Quart. 1, 24–34.

Bryan, L., Joyce, C., 2007. Mobilising Minds: Creating Wealth from Talent in the 21st Century Organization. McGraw Hill, New York.

BT, 2006. Regulatory Report. BT, London.

Bughin, J., Chui, M., Johnson, B., 2008. The next step in open innovation. McKinsey Quart. (June), 34–46.

Burns, J., Baldvinsdottir, G., 2005. An institutional perspective of accountants' new roles – the interplay of contradictions and praxis. Eur. Account. Rev. 14 (4), 725–757.

Busco, C., Giovannoni, E., Riccaboni, A., 2007. Globalisation and the international convergence of management. In: Hopper, T., Northcott, D., Scapens, R. (Eds.), Issues in Management Accounting. Pearson, London, pp. 65–92.

Byrne, J., Brandt, R., Port, O., 1993. The virtual corporation. Business Week 8 (February), 36–41.

Castells, M., 2001. The Internet Galaxy: Reflections on the Internet, Business, and Society. Oxford University Press, Oxford.

Chambers, R.G., 1988. Applied Production Analysis: A Dual Approach. Cambridge University Press, Cambridge.

Chandler, A., Daems, H., 1979. Administrative co-ordination, allocation and monitoring: a comparative analysis of the emergence of accounting and organisations in the USA and Europe. Account. Org. Soc., 3–20.

Chen, S., Dodd, J., 2001. Operating income, residual income and EVA^{TM}: which metric is more value relevant? J. Manag. Issues 13, 65–87.

Chesbrough, H., 2006. Open Business Models. Harvard Business School Press, Boston.

Child, J., 2005. Co-operative Strategy. Oxford University Press, Oxford.

Chow, W.C., Shields, M.D., Wong-Boren, A., 1988. A compilation of recent surveys and a company-specific description of management accounting practices. J. Account. Educ. 6, 183–207.

Chua, W.F., 2007. Accounting, measuring, reporting and strategizing – re-using verbs: a review essay. Account. Org. Soc. 32, 487–494.

CIMA, 2007. CIMA Strategic Scorecard^{TM}: Boards Engaging in Strategy, March, CIMA, London.

Cinquini, L., Tenucci, A., 2007. Is the adoption of strategic management accounting techniques really 'strategy driven'?: evidence from a survey. Conference paper June 18–20, Cost and Performance in Services and Operations, Trento.

Coase, R., 1938. Business organisation and the accounting. The Accountant, issues from October 1 to December 17, reprinted in Solomons, D (ed.) 1968, Studies in Cost Analysis, Sweet & Maxwell, London, pp. 118–133.

Cohen, S.R., Loeb, M., 1982. Public goods, common inputs and the efficiency of full cost allocation. Account. Rev. (April), 336–347.

Colvin, G., 2008. Here it is. Now, you design it! Fortune 26 (May), 16.

Cooper, D.J., Hayes, D., Wolf, F., 1981. Accounting in organized anarchies: understanding and designing accounting systems in ambiguous situations. Account. Org. Soc. 6 (3), 175–191.

Cooper, R., 1987. The two-stage procedure in cost accounting – Part 2. J. Cost Manag. Manuf. Ind. (Summer).

Cooper, R., Kaplan, R.S., 1987. How cost accounting distorts product costs. In: Bruns, W.J., Kaplan, R.S. (Eds.), Accounting and Management: Field Study Perspectives. Harvard Business School Press, Boston, pp. 204–228.

Cooper, R., Slagmulder, R., 2006. Integrated cost management. In: Bhimani, A. (Ed.), Management Accounting: European Perspectives. Oxford University Press, Oxford, pp. 117–145.

Dale, B.G., Plunkett, J., 1999. Quality Costing. Gower, London.

Datar, S., Gupta, M., 1994. Aggregation, specification and measurement errors in product costing. Account. Rev. 69 (4), 559–567.

Dean, J., 1951. Capital Budgeting. Columbia University Press, New York.

Dechow, N., Granlund, M., Mouritsen, J., 2007. Interactions between modern IT and management control. In: Hopper, T., Northcott, D., Scapens, R. (Eds.), Issues in Management Accounting. Pearson, Hemel Hempstead, pp. 45–63.

De Geuser, F., Mooraj, S., Oyon, D., 2008. Does the balanced scorecard add value?: empirical evidence on its effect on performance. Eur. Account. Rev. (October), 1–30.

Dixon, R., 1998. Accounting for strategic management: a practical application. Long Range Planning 31 (2), 272–279.

Drori, G., Meyer, J., 2006. Global scientisation: an environment for expanded organization. In: Drori, G., Meyer, J., Hwang, H. (Eds.), Globalisation and Organization: World Society and Organizational Change. Oxford University Press, Oxford, pp. 50–68.

Drury, C., Braund, S., Osborne, P., Tayles, M., 1993. A Survey of Management Accounting Practice in UK Manufacturing Companies. Chartered Association of Certified Accountants, London.

Dugdale, D., Jones, C., Green, S., 2006. Contemporary Management Accounting Practices in UK Manufacturing. Elsevier/CIMA, London.

Edwards, J.R., Boyns, T., 2006. The development of cost and management accounts in Britain. In: Chapman, C.S., Hopwood, A.G., Shields, M.D. (Eds.), Handbook of Management Accounting Research, vol. 2. Elsevier, Oxford, pp. 969–1034.

Ernst & Young, 2003. 2003 Survey of Management Accounting. Ernst & Young LLP/Institute of Management Accountants, SCORE Retrieval File No.BV0008.

Ezzamel, M., Hoskin, K.W., Macve, R.H., 1990. Managing it all by numbers: a review of Johnson & Kaplan's *Relevance Lost*. Account. Bus. Res. 20 (7), 153–166.

Faulhaber, G.R., 1975. Cross subsidization: pricing in public enterprise. Am. Econ. Rev., 966–977.

Fleischmann, R., Tyson, T., 2006. The history of management accounting in the US. In: Chapman, C.S., Hopwood, A.G., Shields, M.D. (Eds.), Handbook of Management Accounting Research, vol. 2. Elsevier, Oxford, pp. 1071–1090.

Ford, H., 2008. From portals to platforms. WBS J. (July–September), 45–47.

Fortt, J., 2008. Michael Dell friends his customers. Fortune 15 (September), 18–22.

Garcke, E., Fells, J., 1887. Factory Accounts: Their Principles and Practice. Crosby Lockwood, London.

Gosselin, M., 2006. A review of activity-based costing: technique, implementation, and consequences. In: Chapman, C.S., Hopwood, A.G., Shields, M.D. (Eds.), Handbook of Management Accounting Research, vol. 2. Elsevier, Oxford, pp. 641–673.

Gould, J.R., 1962. The economist's cost concept and business problems. In: Baxter, W.T., Davidson, S. (Eds.), Studies in Accounting Theory. Sweet & Maxwell, London, pp. 218–235.

Gould, J.R., 1964. Internal pricing in firms where there are costs of using an outside market. J. Bus. (January), 61–67.

Granlund, M., Malmi, T., 2002. Moderate impact of ERPS on management accounting: a lag or permanent outcome? Manag. Account. Res. 13 (3), 299–321.

Guilding, C., McManus, I., 2002. The incidence, perceived merit and antecedents of customer accounting: an exploratory note. Account. Org. Soc. 27, 45–59.

Guilding, C., Lamminmaki, D., Drury, C., 1998. Budgeting and standard costing practices in New Zealand and the United Kingdom. Int. J. Account. 33 (5), 569–588.

Guilding, C., Cravens, K.S., Tayles, M., 2000. An international comparison of strategic management accounting practices. Manag. Account. Res. 11 (1), 113–135.

Gulati, R., 2007. Silobusting: how to execute on the promise of customer focus. Harvard Business Review. Harvard Business School Press, Boston.

Hall, G., Rosenthal, J. Wade, J., 1994. How to make re-engineering really work. Turnaround Management Association. <http://www.turnaround.org/Publications/Articles.aspx?objectID=2070>.

Hallowell, R., 2002. Virtuous Cycles: Improving Service and Lowering Costs in E-Commerce HBS Note -802-169.

Hansen, A., Mouritsen, J., 2007. Management accounting and changing operations management. In: Hopper, T., Northcott, D., Scapens, R. (Eds.), Issues in Management Accounting. Pearson, London.

Harmon, 2009. Viewed 26 March 2009. <http://www.business.com/directory/industrialHarmon(2009)goods&services/machinery&tools/industrialautomation/flexible_manufacturing_systems>.

Haskett, J., Sasser, W., Schesinger, L., 1997. The Service Profit Chain. Free Press, New York.

Hess, H., 1903. Manufacturing: capital, costs, profit and dividends. Eng. Mag. (December).

Hippel, vonE., 2005. Democratizing Innovation. MIT Press, Cambridge, MA.

Hirschleifer, J., 1956. On the economics of transfer pricing. J. Bus. (July), 172–184.

Hirschleifer, J., 1957. Economics of the divisionalised firm. J. Bus. 5 (April), 96–108.

Hope, J., Fraser, R., 2003. Beyond Budgeting: How Managers Can Break Free from the Annual Performance Trap. Harvard Business Press, Boston, MA.

Hopwood, A.G., 1983. On trying to study accounting in the contexts in which it operates. Account. Org. Soc. 8, 207–305.

Hopwood, A.G., 2009. Accounting and the environment. Account. Org. Soc. 34 (3/4), 433–439.

Hopwood, A.G., Miller, P., 1994. Accounting as Social and Institutional Practice. Cambridge University Press, Cambridge, UK.

Hoque, Z., 2006. Strategic Management Accounting. Butterworth-Heinemann, London.

Horngren, C.T., 1962. Cost Accounting: A Managerial Emphasis. Prentice Hall, Englewood Cliffs.

Hoskin, K., Macve, R., 1986. Accounting and the examination: a geneology of disciplinary power. Account. Org. Soc. 11 (2), 105–136.

Hoskin, K., Macve, R., Stone, J., 2006. Accounting and strategy: towards understanding the historical genesis of modern and military accounting strategy. In: Bhimani, A. (Ed.), Management Accounting: European Perspectives. Oxford University Press, Oxford, pp. 166–197.

Information Age. 2008. Valentino's Designer ERP Information Age. 21 May. P. 12.

IFAC, 2005. The Roles and Domain of the Professional Accountant in Business. International Federation of Accountants, New York.

Institute of Management Accountants, 2007. Enterprise Risk Management: Tools and Techniques for Effective Implementation. IMA, Montvale, NJ.

Innes, J., Mitchell, F., Sinclair, D., 2000. Activity-based costing in the UK largest companies: a comparison of 1994 and 1999 survey results. Manag. Account. Res. 11, 349–362.

Istvan, D.F., 1961. Capital Expenditure Decisions: How They Are Made in Large Corporations. Foundation for Economic and Business Decisions, Bloomington.

Jaedicke, R.K., Robichek, A.A., 1964. Cost–volume–profit analysis under conditions of uncertainty. Account. Rev. 39 (4), 917–926.

Jönsson, P.W., 2006. Value-Based Management – Positioning of Claimed Merits and Analysis of Application. Lund Business Press, Lund.

Johnson, H.T., 1983. The search for gain in markets and firms: a review of the historical emergence of management accounting systems. Account. Org. Soc. 8 (1), 139–146.

Johnson, H.T., Kaplan, R.S., 1987. Relevance Lost: The Rise and Fall of Management Accounting. Harvard Business School Press, Boston, MA.

Jordon, J.P., Harris, G.L., 1920. Cost Accounting: Principles and Practice. The Ronald Press Company, New York.

Kaplan, R.S., Norton, D.P., 1992. The balanced scorecard – measures that drive performance. Harvard Business Review. Harvard Business School Press, Boston, 70 (1), 71–79.

Kaplan, R.S., Norton, D.P., 1996. The Balanced Scorecard – Translating Strategy into Action. Harvard Business School Press, Boston.

Kaplan, R.S., Norton, D.P., 2008. Mastering the management system. Harvard Business Review. Harvard Business School Press, Boston, January, pp. 62–77.

Kianni, R., Sangeladji, M., 2003. An empirical study about the use of ABC/ABM models by some Fortune 500 largest industrial corporations in the USA. J. Am. Acad. Bus. 3, 689–713.

Kim, H.Y, 1987. Economies of scale in multi-product firms: an empirical analysis. Economica 54 (214), 185–206 New series.

Kurunmaki, L., Miller, P., 2006. Modernizing government: the calculating self, hybridization and performance measurement. In: Bhimani, A. (Ed.), Management Accounting: European Perspectives. Oxford University Press, Oxford, pp. 198–216.

Labro, E., Vanhoucke, M., 2007. A simulation analysis of interactions among errors in costing systems. Account. Rev. 82 (4), 939–962.

Langfield-Smith, K., 2008. Strategic management accounting: how far have we come in 25 years? Account. Audit. Account. J. 2 (2), 204–228.

Lipe, M.G., Salterio, S., 2002. A note on the judgmental effects of the balanced scorecard's information organization. Account. Org. Soc. 27 (5), 531–540.

Loft, A., 1990. Coming into the Light. CIMA, London.

Lord, B.R., 1996. Strategic management accounting: the emperor's new clothes? Manag. Account. Res. 7 (3), 347–366.

McKinsey, 2008. How finance departments are changing. McKinsey Quart. 5 (April), 2–9.

Major, M., 2007. Activity-based costing and management: a critical review. In: Hopper, T., Northcott, D., Scapens, R. (Eds.) Issues in Management Accounting. Pearson, London, pp. 155–173.

Manes, R., 1966. A new dimension to breakeven analysis. J. Account. Res. 4 (1 Spring), 87–102.

Manyika, J., Roberts, R., Sprague, K., 2008. Eight business technology trends to watch. McKinsey Quart., 60–71.

Mennicken, A., 2002. Bringing calculation back in: sociological studies in accounting. Economic Sociol. 3 (3), 17–27.

Merchant, K., Van der Stede, W., 2007. Management Control Systems: Performance Measurement, Evaluation and Incentives. Pearson, London.

Merrett, A.J., Sykes, A., 1963. The Finance and Analysis of Capital Projects. Longmans, London.

Mikes, A., 2009. Risk management and calculative cultures. Manag. Account. Res. 20 (1), 18–40.

Miller, P., O'Leary, T., 1987. Accounting and the construction of the governable person. Account. Org. Soc. 12 (3), 235–265.

Miller, P., O'Leary, T., 1994. Accounting, 'economic citizenship' and the spatial reordering of manufacture. Account. Org. Soc. 19 (1), 15–43.

Miller, P.B., O'Leary, T., 2005. Capital budgeting, coordination and strategy: a field study of interfirm and intrafirm mechanisms. In: Chapman, C.S. (Ed.), Controlling Strategy – Management, Accounting, and Performance Measurement. Oxford University Press, Oxford, pp. 151–182.

Mintzberg, H., 1989. Inside our Strange World of Organizations. Free Press, New York.

Mowshowitz, A., 1994. Virtual organization: a vision of management in the information age. Inform. Soc. 10 (4), 267–288.

Mouritsen, J., Hansen, A., 2006. Management accounting, operations, and network relations: debating the lateral dimension. In: Bhimani, A. (Ed.), Management Accounting: European Perspectives. Oxford University Press, Oxford, pp. 266–290.

Nagumo, T., Donlon, B.S., 2006. Integrating the balanced scorecard and COSO ERM framework. Cost Management July/August 2006, pp. 20–30.

Noreen, E., 1991. Conditions under which activity-based costing systems provide relevant costs. J. Manag. Account. Res. 3, 159–168.

Noreen, E., Soderstrom, N., 1994. Are overhead costs strictly proportional to activity? Evidence from hospital services departments. J. Account.Econ. (17), 255–278.

Noreen, E., Soderstrom, N., 1997. The accuracy of proportional cost models: evidence from hospital service departments. Rev. Account. Stud. 2, 89–114.

Norreklit, H., 2003. The balanced scorecard: what is the score: a rhetorical analysis of the balanced scorecard. Account. Org. Soc. 28 (6), 591–619.

Norreklit, H., Mitchell, F., 2007. The balanced scorecard. In: Hopper, T., Northcott, D., Scapens, R. (Eds.), Issues in Management Accounting. Pearson, London, pp. 175–196.

Otley, D., 2006. Trends in budgetary control and responsibility accounting. In: Bhimani, A. (Ed.), Management Accounting: European Perspectives. Oxford University Press, Oxford, pp. 291–307.

Power, M., 2007. Organised Uncertainty: Designing a World of Risk Management. Oxford University Press, Oxford.

Prahalad, C.K., Krishnan, M.S., 2008. The New Age of Innovation: Driving Co-created Value Through Global Networks. McGraw Hill, New York.

Preinreich, G., 1938. Annual studies of economic theory: the theory of depreciation. Econometrica 5 (July), 219–241.

Rigby, D., 2007. Executive Guide – Management Tools 2007. Bain & Company Publishing. <www.bain.com/management tools/Management Tools and Trends 2007.pdf>.

Reichelstein, S., 2000. Providing managerial incentives: cash flows versus accrual accounting. J. Account. Res. 38, 243–270.

Roberts, H., 2006. Making management accounting intelligible. In: Bhimani, A. (Ed.), Contemporary Issues in Management Accounting. Oxford University Press, Oxford, pp. 308–327.

Rogerson, W.P., 1997. Inter-temporal cost allocation and managerial investment incentives: a theory explaining the use of economic value added as a performance measure. J. Polit. Econ. 44, 770–795.

Roslender, R., Hart, S., 2003. In search of strategic management accounting: theoretical and field study perspectives. Manag. Account. Res. 14, 255–279.

Sako, M., 1992. Prices, Quality and Trust. Cambridge University Press, Cambridge.

Scapens, R., 2006. Changing times: management accounting research and practice from a UK perspective. In: Bhimani, A. (Ed.), Management Accounting: European Perspectives. Oxford University Press, Oxford, pp. 329–354.

Shank, J.K., 2006. Strategic cost management: upsizing, downsizing and right(?) sizing. In: Bhimani, A. (Ed.), Contemporary Issues in Management Accounting. Oxford University Press, Oxford, pp. 355–379.

Shank, J.K., Govindarajan, V., 1993. Strategic Cost Management. The Free Press, New York.

Sharkey, W.A., 1989. The Theory of Natural Monopoly. Cambridge University Press, Cambridge.

Shillinglaw, G., 1963. The Concept of Attributable Cost. J. Account. Res. 1 (1 Spring), 73–85.

Simmonds, K., 1981. Strategic management accounting. Manag. Account. (April), 26–29.

Simon, H.H., Guetzkow, G., Tyndall, G., 1954. Centralization Vs Decentralisation in Organizing the Controller's Department. Controllership Foundation, New York.

Solomons, D., 1965. Divisional Performance: Measurement and Control. Financial Executive Research Foundation, New York.

Solomons, D., 1968. Studies in Cost Analysis. Sweet & Maxwell, London.

Soonawalla, K., 2006. Environmental management accounting in. In: Bhimani, A. (Ed.), Management Accounting: European Perspectives. Oxford University Press, Oxford, pp. 380–406.

Stern Jr., J.M., Stewart, G., Chew, H., 1995. The EVA financial management system. J. Appl. Corp. Finance 8 (Summer), 32–46.

Straub, D.W., 2004. Foundations of Net-Enhanced Organizations. John Wiley & Sons, Hoboken.

Tapscott, D., 2009. Grown Up Digital: How the Net Generation is Changing Your World. McGraw Hill, New York.

Thomas, A.L., 1969. The allocation problem in financial accounting theory. Account. Res. Study (3) American Accounting Association.

Thomas, A.L., 1974. The allocation problem: part two. Account. Res. Study (9) American Accounting Association.

Tillmann, K., Goddard, A., 2008. Strategic management accounting and sense-making in a large multinational company. Manag. Account. Res. 19, 80–102.

Tor, J.K., 1996. R&D scope economies and plant performance. RAND J. Econ. 27 (3 Autumn), 502–522.

Treadway, M., Rogers, S., Spencer, L., Stewart, S. 2005. The Agile CFO: Acting on Business Insight. IBM Global Business Services, December.

Vaivio, J., 1999. Exploring a "non-financial" management accounting change. Management Accounting Research, 10, 409–437.

Vaivio, J., 2007. Examining the 'quantified' customer. Account. Org. Soc. 24 (8), 689–715.

Varian, H.R., 2006. Intermediate Microeconomics: A Modern Approach. WW Norton & Co, New York.

Ward, K., 1997. Strategic Management Accounting. Butterworth-Heinemann, London.

Willsmore, A.W., 1931. Business Budgets and Budgetary Control. Sir Isaac Pitman, London.

Index

Economic crisis, 19–20, 20, 89–91
Economic depreciation, 27
Economic order quantity, 63
Economic value-added approach, 8, 11, 107
Economies
multi-product, 45, 108
of scale, 41–43, 108
of scope, 41–46, 108
Electronic media, 105
Engineers, 2
Enterprise Governance Framework, 87
Enterprise resource planning (ERP), 53, 64–67
road-maps, 65
Enterprise Risk Management (ERM), 71, 72
ERM. *See* Enterprise Risk Management
ERP. *See* Enterprise resource planning
External failures, 61

F
Facebook, 81, 83, 84
Factory Accounts: Their Principles and Practice (Garcke and Fells), 2
Failure
external, 61
internal, 61
non-comformance, 59–60
FASB. *See* Financial Accounting Standards Board
Field repair, 59
Finance department, re-engineering of, 14–15
Finance function, 77–79
Financial Accounting Standards Board (FASB), 91
Financial Crisis Advisory Group, 91
Financial Services Authority, 91
Financial transactions, 91
Fixed costs, 2, 26
Flexibility, 54–56
Flexible automation, 67–69
Flexible manufacturing systems (FMSs), 54, 67
decision to use, 68
Flexible organisational technologies (FOTs), 53, 56–69
quality, 57–62
Flexible technologies, 53–75

Flikster, 81, 84
Fluid organisations, 53–75
FMSs. *See* Flexible manufacturing systems
Ford, 74
FOTs. *See* Flexible organisational technologies
Fully-fledged value management approach, 12
Functional costing, 55

G
GAAP. *See* Generally accepted accounting principles
Gap, 69
GBS. *See* Global Business Services
General Electric, 8, 11
Generally accepted accounting principles (GAAP), 11
Gillette, 89
Global Business Services (GBS), 73, 78
Globalisation, 20, 69–70, 77–94
complexities, 103
Google, 86
Googlemail, 84
Great Depression, 90
Grove, Andy, 89

H
HDTV, 56
Herz, Robert, 91
High quality/low price, 79–80
Hugo Bass, 66
Hybrid accountants, 104

I
IASB. *See* International Accounting Standards Board
IBM, 15, 82
ICMA. *See* Institute of Cost and Management Accountants
ICWA. *See* Institute of Cost and Management Works Accountants
Ideal product cost, 40n3
IdeaStorm, 74
IFAC. *See* International Federation of Accountants
IFRS. *See* International Financial Reporting Standards